Motivational Hypnotism

Motivational Hypnotism

Fiona Biddle

and

Shaun Brookhouse

UK Academy of Therapeutic Arts and Sciences Ltd.

Motivational Hypnotism

Published by

UK Academy of Therapeutic Arts and Sciences Ltd
16 St Philips Rd, Burton on the Wolds, Loughborough, LE12 5TS
Tel: 01509 881811
Email: info@ukacademy.org
Internet: www.ukacademy.org

ISBN 0-9544604-1-3

Note

Neither the publishers nor the authors will be liable for any loss or damage of any nature occasioned to or suffered by any person acting or refraining from acting as a result of reliance on the material contained in this publication.

Printed in the UK by Lightning Source

Dedication

We would like to dedicate this book to all those who have motivated us through our years in this profession:

I would like to thank my husband Stuart for his constant support, patience and for providing much of the information used in the "Theories of Motivation" chapter. I thank my sons, Jack and Greg for their love, which inspires me and I also wish to thank Shaun: he has encouraged me to stretch myself further than I could have imagined.

Fiona

I would like to dedicate this book to my wife Elizabeth, whose patience with regards to my work seems boundless, my dear friend and co-author Fiona whose knowledge never fails to impress me and my dog Brewster and my rabbit Cottontail, because they bring me happiness and take my mind off the rigor of work. Finally, I would like to dedicate this to all of the hypnotists I have trained over the years, as they have taught me at least as much as I have taught them.

Shaun

Note: the names used in our Case Examples are not the clients' real names: all names represent someone (in some cases more than one person) who is important to us, sometimes directly, sometimes obscurely. Perhaps you can find yourself there!

Contents

About the Authors

Fiona Biddle

BSc, DipCouns, DipCAH, HPD, BCH, FNCH

Fiona has been in professional practice since 1993. She is a Board Certified Hypnotist, a Certified Instructor with the National Guild of Hypnotists, and received the President's Award from the National Guild of Hypnotists in 2004. She is also a humanistic counsellor and coach with a particular interest in the fulfilment of potential.

In addition to her therapeutic work, Fiona is also Executive Director of the National Council for Hypnotherapy (UK) and Principal of the UK Academy of Therapeutic Arts and Sciences. She has co-written a number of therapeutic course manuals and has published another book with Shaun Brookhouse; Building a Successful and Ethical Therapy Practice.

Shaun Brookhouse

GCGI, MA, DCH, PhD, CertEd, PGDHP, DipProfCouns, HPD, FNGH, FNCH

Shaun has been in professional practice since 1989. He is an award winning hypnotherapist, receiving some of the most prestigious honours and Fellowships in the profession, including the Rexford L North Memorial Trophy for Life Time Achievement from the National Guild of Hypnotists.

Shaun is a Board Certified Hypnotist, a Certified Master Instructor with the National Guild of Hypnotists, a past Chairman of the National Council for Hypnotherapy (UK), a UKCP Registered Psychotherapist, and a NLP Master Trainer. He is the Director of Brookhouse Hypnotherapy Ltd, Principal of the Washington School of Clinical and Advanced Hypnosis, and Director of Education of the UK Academy of Therapeutic Arts and Sciences.

Shaun and Fiona have co-developed the S to the Third Power Hypnotism System.

Foreword

I am delighted to have been asked to write the foreword of this book. Having been practising hypnotism since the late 1940s, my colleague, Dr John Hughes, and I conducted hypnotism training and motivational seminars throughout the U.S. starting during our college days in the mid 1950s. These were somewhat different to the model presented in this book, but there were, and always will be, eager students interested in learning more about this fascinating subject.

Over the years, as president of the oldest and largest hypnotism organization in the world, The National Guild of Hypnotists, I have been talking about the "Big Idea", which is to see hypnotism become a separate and distinct profession in its own right -the time finally arrived in the year 2005. There have been many advances bringing us to this goal, one of which is this authoritative work on the principles and application of motivational theory within a hypnotic practice.

The authors of this text, Fiona Biddle and Shaun Brookhouse, have embraced "The Big Idea". They have worked for over 28 years combined to help this field in becoming the profession that it is today. As practitioners, instructors and authors, they have done much in their home country to bring about better recognition of hypnotism, having helped set up the first UK nationally accredited qualification open to all hypnotists, and National Occupational Standards. In addition, they are very active within the National Guild of Hypnotists and have been instrumental in helping us to bring the standards of hypnotic education up to a level of which the profession can be proud.

I thoroughly recommend this text for both experienced and novice hypnotists. If you read and utilize the material contained in this work, it can only help you to take your hypnotism practice to the next level.

Dwight F Damon, DC, FNGH
President
National Guild of Hypnotists
PO Box 308
Merrimack, New Hampshire 03054

Introduction

Who should read this book?

This book is designed for use by professional hypnotists or hypnotherapists, or those in training. Others with an interest in hypnotism, psychology or psychotherapy may also find it to be relevant, but the techniques should not be practised without being suitably qualified (see p181, Ethical Practice).

We use the terms "hypnotist" in this book, rather than "hypnotherapist", as the latter term is specifically outlawed in some areas of the world, particularly some states of the USA. We are aware that this may cause some confusion, particularly in the UK, where it is common to use the term "hypnotist" to refer to a "stage hypnotist" and "hypnotherapist" for one using hypnosis for change work. It was a decision that could not please everybody so if you are one of those who prefer to use "hypnotherapist", please be assured that this process **is** the process that we are discussing.

We did consider using the term "professional hypnotist" throughout, but this seemed a little excessive, and perhaps superfluous as we are keen to demonstrate a professional and ethical approach to hypnotism throughout the book.

Another area of confusion in terminology is the difference between "hypnosis" and "hypnotism". In this book, we take "hypnosis" to be the state that is induced, and "hypnotism" to be the process; the equivalent of the term hypnotherapy.

Why read this book?

Much of the work of hypnotists revolves around dealing with problems, helping clients to resolve issues and to make changes. It is often said that most clients want to stop doing something they do or start doing something they are not doing. While this area of hypnotism is fascinating and extremely beneficial, to see the profession only in this way is limiting.

All hypnotism courses cover methods of working with problems, including suggestion and age regression but often they concentrate on the negative. For example, there are schools that say that a client experiencing anxiety must go back into their past and re-experience events which caused the anxiety. Some insist that these events be re-lived with all the trauma associated, while others say that the experience can be viewed from a dissociated vantage point. We will discuss these schools of thought in more detail in the section, Analytical Hypnotism. See p45.

All courses also cover working with some areas that could be construed as positive, such as habit breaking and confidence, but often, once again from a less than positive viewpoint. This book is for you if you want to increase the positive aspects of your work, wherever possible.

It is also for you if you want to increase your marketability by adding new areas of expertise to your practice. In our experience, the vast majority of people who contact a hypnotist through the usual means, that is, deciding that they want help and seeking a person suitably qualified in their area, will do so because of a problem that they are suffering with.

You have an opportunity to put yourself out into the marketplace in a positive way, which we will be discussing in the Marketing chapter, so that clients who have never even considered hypnotism as an option in their situation, will call you.

What will this book cover?

It is very important that any practical application is based on sound theory. Therefore this book is split into two distinct sections, theory and practice. If you get excited by theory, the first section, we hope, will give you sufficient detail to get a good understanding of the theories, both of motivation and hypnotism that support our model. If, however, you are the type of person who would rather just get on with the "doing", we have given short synopses of the theories that will be sufficient ground for you to use the practical chapters.

The practical section is divided into topics, and in each we will show you how you can apply the theory as discussed. Some ideas on how to create suggestions and scripts will be included, but our ethos is that scripts, while useful starting points, can hamper innovation and stifle creativity. Therefore we encourage you to develop your style of work, based on solid knowledge, and trusting in your own unconscious mind to work in the way that produces the most effective interventions.

The book then covers some areas where special consideration should be given, a discussion and some ideas on how to market your practice as a Motivational Hypnotist, and finally some thoughts on future directions: this is a new concept and one that we hope will develop and grow.

How to use this book

People vary widely on how they read books. Most read novels from start to finish (but not all!), but there is no need to do so with a text book such as this unless you want to. We suggest that you read through the theory chapters, perhaps just reading the synopses to start with. You can then read the detail if this interests you, but you will be ready to move on to the practical applications.

Again you can read through the practical section from start to finish if you choose, or dip in, perhaps when a client rings with a particular request. In this way you can gain experience in being a Motivational Hypnotist before specifically marketing yourself in this way.

Please check through the areas of special consideration, see p180, so that you are prepared for these eventualities.

After a while, you will then be ready to immerse yourself in the Marketing chapter, so that you can build your practice with your new specialism.

Theories of Motivation

There are many theories of motivation. Here we will highlight a few, and create a framework for understanding how these theories can be utilised in assisting clients to meet their objectives (whatever they are) with hypnotism.

We have the following specific objectives for this chapter:

- To define motivation and its subcomponents
- To outline, briefly, historical trends in the study of human motivation, as well as principles for a general theory of motivation so that hypnotism practice can be based on solid ground
- To discuss descriptive approaches to motivation and identification of barriers to success
- To comment on other determinants, such as self-motivation and control

Change is rarely easy. If it is, then clients make the changes themselves without the need of a hypnotist. Therefore hypnotists only ever see clients who are struggling to make the change they desire. There are not only the obvious psychological factors that have an influence, but also social, environmental and biological influences. As we will see in the chapter on Theories of Hypnotism, it is common to ignore these factors and presume that only the psychological, or emotional level is relevant. We will show how our model utilises motivational theories to enhance the chances of change, not only being made, but significantly, maintained.

Definition of motivation

We will use Maehr and Braskamp's (1986) components of motivation as an operational definition. Motivation is often considered to be a combination of direction and intensity, but the Maehr and Braskamp view is more detailed. They state that "most motivational talk arises from observations about variation in five behavioural patterns, which we label direction, persistence, continuing motivation, intensity and performance (Maehr and Braskamp 1986). We will concentrate on the first four of these, as performance (ie judging a person's motivation by how well they perform) is not as relevant in our domain as in others.

Direction

The first indicator of motivation is that of direction. This is the behaviour of focus that implies a choice has been made, or is being made and so decision making is central to understanding motivation. For example, a smoking client has made a choice to stop, which they are unable (or believe they are unable) to implement on their own. Another example might be a client who has decided that they are unhappy to continue with their current level of stress and is thus motivated in the direction of stress reduction. Choice is not always obvious, and alternative behaviours should be considered. If our smoking client believes that to quit would mean putting on weight, this could affect their motivation, and our stress client would need to consider alternative ways of being rather than simply being "less stressed". This may be more relaxed or more confident while continuing with the situations which created the stress, or to alter those situations (or a combination of both).

Choice is also an interesting question in terms of belief and whether choices are made at a conscious or unconscious level. Many smokers perceive themselves not to have a choice as to whether they have a cigarette, and yet struggle little when they are not able to smoke (eg on a plane). Choice can be seen as a continuum with absolute choice at one end, and no choice at all at the other. Where a client believes that they are on this continuum will affect the possibility of success, and motivation can be increased by encouraging movement along the continuum towards choice.

Direction may be broadly towards an outcome that is perceived as beneficial, or away from an outcome that is seen as negative. Interventions are most effective when they address both. For example, a client who says they wish to stop smoking to avoid disease can strengthen their motivation by gaining awareness of the positive aspects of being a non-smoker.

In some models of motivation the direction element is defined as the pain/pleasure principal, stating that we are motivated towards pleasure and away from pain. While we feel that this model has merit, it is too simplistic for most clients that a hypnotist will see in their consulting room.

Persistence

Maehr and Braskamp's second factor, persistence refers to the degree of sustained concentration on one task. A lack of persistence may be demonstrated by a weight control client who starts to walk to work and gives up after five minutes, or another who sticks to a healthy eating plan all day and then binges on chocolate in the evening. Choice and decision making are critical here too and are likely to be correlated with the perceived value of success. This shows the importance of working to maximise the impact of the clients value system on the choice they are making.

Continuing motivation

The third factor is continuing motivation. This differs from persistence in that it relates to the need for motivation to continue long term, maybe after some sort of relapse. Lets look at the three examples we have looked at so far. Perhaps the smoker gets drunk at a party and has a cigarette. Continuing motivation would result in him continuing as a non-smoker from the following morning. Our stress client has made excellent progress in coping better with her stressors and finding activities that are important which are not stressful. She has a setback in that there is a particularly stressful situation at work and she feels she does not cope well. If she does not have continuing motivation to be a less stressed person she could slip back into old patterns. Finally our weight control client goes on holiday to a hotel where meals are provided and eats far more than he had been doing, and a lot of the wrong things. The scales show he has put on 4 pounds. Continuing motivation would mean that he puts this down to experience and gets back to his healthy eating plan on return from holiday.

Intensity

The fourth factor in motivation is intensity, or how much one is motivated. The relevance of intensity relates to the difficulty of the change that is required. Difficulty, however, is hard to define or predict. It is often related to how much a person's identity is entwined with the behaviour or way of being. For example, people who perceive themselves as "smokers" are likely to find it harder to change, and therefore need a higher intensity of motivation to quit than those who perceive themselves as "people who smoke". Similarly, take two women who want to lose weight. One tells you that she has always been fat, and the other tells you that she has always been slim, until the last year when she starting eating business lunches. Who will probably need a greater intensity of motivation? Yes, probably the one whose identity (being fat) needs to change along with behaviours.

Definition of motivation

Direction: towards the positive or away from the negative

Persistence: sticking to a task

Continuing motivation: long term motivation

Intensity: strength of the desire for change

Approaches to motivation

Following on from this model, we can now look at two types of approach to the study of motivation. These types are descriptive and theoretical.

Descriptive approach

This approach uses self-reported perceived reasons for behaviour or change. It is a surface level approach and is thus limited in scope. All hypnotists will recognise the fact that what a client gives as the reason for change is not necessarily the real or only reason. This may be within the client's awareness or not.

This approach, however, can give a considerable amount of information that while not necessarily "accurate", is useful, particularly in the area of perceived barriers to success. In this context, perception is critical, and this gives great scope for working on the individual's motivation.

> **Descriptive approach**
>
> **The descriptive approach is used to find out the client's perceptions about their motivation and situation, and gives useful background information on beliefs and values.**

For example, a 25 year old smoker may report that their motivation to quit is because they saw a government warning on television about the dangers of smoking. This is likely to be a surface level motivation as no 25 year old smoker would have been unaware of the risks before seeing the advert. The hypnotist's job is to expand on this and drill down further to find and enhance all their inner motivations.

An example of a descriptive barrier may be the weight control client who says she cannot lose weight because she works in a school shop that sells sweets and chocolate. This gives good scope to work using the theoretical models that we will come to shortly to help her to get around this barrier.

Theoretical approaches

Theoretical approaches to the study of motivation seek to explain and understand the basis of an individual's motivation in order to be able to work with this to maximise motivation for a successful outcome.

Theories can be divided into four types, although there is quite a lot of overlap between them. The four categories are Control, Competence, Beliefs, and Decision Making.

Control

Two of the key approaches which emphasise control as a motivational factor are Rotter's Locus of Control theory, and attribution theory. Both recognise the importance of the perception of control and expectations. It is also an important factor in models of intrinsic motivation and can help explain individual differences. Autonomy is also a factor linked to the idea of control.

Expectancy-value theories make the assumption that people's behaviour is guided logically by the anticipated consequences of the behaviour (expectancies) and the value or importance they attach to such outcomes. Whether, and to what degree, we actually make such decisions is debatable and variable but there is a role for such theories. Perhaps they expect humans to be too logical and rational.

It is obvious to any hypnotist that the need to take control is associated with many decisions that clients take to change. Many want to "take charge", and stop being controlled by cigarettes, food, anxiety, old trauma, other people etc. Going too far down the "control" line can be counter-productive with some clients, however. If the client feels they are being told that they have control it can be interpreted as blame in having been "out of control" before. There is a fine line to be drawn between responsibility and blame.

Skinner (1995) proposes a 'competence system' model. We include this here, rather than in the 'Competence' section as it comprises the various parts that help to explain control. This model analyses the relationship between the components agent (the person), means (behaviour) and ends (outcomes) in conjunction with belief systems. There are various combinations of these factors:

Agent, means and capacity beliefs: belief that the person has the means to produce the desired behaviour (but not necessarily an outcome), ie confidence in the process.

Means, ends and strategy beliefs: belief that adopting a particular strategy will produce the expected outcome.

Agent, ends and control beliefs: belief that the self can control the outcome. This involves both capacity and strategy beliefs.

Locus of Control

Locus of control stems from a social learning theory approach to personality where general beliefs are thought to develop from expectations based on prior reinforcements and hence is an expectancy-value approach to motivation. Expectancy-value means that it is looking at a combination of both elements: the expectancy of a particular outcome and the value of the outcome. For example, imagine a group of overweight people. Some may have a high expectancy that if they were to walk for half an hour a day, they would lose weight. Others would not. Some would value losing weight highly, others would not. Those who are high in both have the greatest chance of success.

Locus of control of reinforcements refers to the extent to which people perceive that reinforcements are within their own control, are controlled by others or are due to chance. Rotter says "it seems likely that, depending on the individual's history of reinforcement, individuals would differ to the degree to which they attributed reinforcements to their own actions' (Rotter, 1966).

There are psychometric tests which can determine an individual's tendency towards an internal or external locus of control. For our purpose, it is important to recognise that the client's specific locus of control with respect to the issue that they are presenting can be a significant factor in our process of helping a client maximise their motivation, and perhaps their overall tendency is irrelevant: the hypnotist needs to know where the client is right now, with respect to the issue they are in the office to work on. If their overall tendency is more beneficial than the specific, however, then mapping techniques could be used to increase the benefit of the specific.

It is generally perceived that having an internal locus of control is "good" and external is "bad". However, this is not always the case. For example, a client may, as a child have felt responsible for her parents' arguments. This is an internal LOC, and part of the motivational hypnotist's role here may be, in this one instance, to shift this so that she knows that this is not within her control, but to help her to see that she can have control of how she now responds.

Control

The control theories look at whether the person feels they can control their behaviour and/or the outcome of that behaviour.

Locus of Control is the term used to describe a tendency to presume control to be internal to the self or external. Eg "I determine my results" or "it's all down to fate"

Both the client's general tendency and how they feel about the specific issue are important.

So how does feeling in control fit the process of motivation? It is clear from everyday life that most of us, most of the time are more motivated by situations which involve choice, control and self-determination. Conversely most of us, most of the time, prefer not to be controlled or pressured too much. These ideas bring us to the concept of intrinsic and extrinsic motivation.

Intrinsic motivation is being motivated by the process itself, usually for fun, enjoyment, challenge etc. Intrinsic motivation is often considered to be key in persistence and continuing motivation. However there are few situations that hypnotists will face where the motivation is truly intrinsic (smokers do not quit because they enjoy the process of becoming a non-smoker, and a phobic client will not be motivated to resolve their issue by the thought of the fun of systematic desensitisation!). However, where possible these elements can be built on. Also, as you extend your practice as a Motivational Hypnotist, you can attract clients for issues where this is more of a factor, such as in performance and personal development areas.

Deci and Ryan (1985) suggest that there are four approaches to intrinsic motivation: free choice, interest, challenge and 'needs'. These needs include 'relatedness', 'competence' and 'self-determination'. This suggests that if a change or behaviour is of the person's choice, is interesting, is a challenge, and meets one or more of these needs, the person is more likely to be motivated than not. All of these are areas that can be examined by the hypnotist and client together, and maximised.

Intrinsic Motivation

This is being motivated by the process itself, typically for interest, challenge or enjoyment.

There are also three needs that may be met by intrinsic motivation:

- **relatedness**
- **competence**
- **autonomy**

Extrinsic motivation is that which is external to the process and is most typically seen as rewards. Deci and Ryan interestingly suggest that increasing extrinsic motivation is not necessarily a good thing as it can lead to a decrease in intrinsic motivation. This fact was backed up by research conducted with school children. The children were divided into three groups to play with brightly coloured pens; one group were told they would be rewarded (and were), the second group were told nothing, but were also rewarded, and the third did not receive an award. The experiment showed that the children who had been told they would be rewarded for playing with, subsequently played with them significantly less than the other children. This shows that it is the expectation of reward that can be an issue.

Reward is not the only form of extrinsic motivation however. It may also include approval and pressure for example. Deci and Ryan's 'self-determination theory' (drawn from the needs stated above), divides this into four aspects or 'reasons' for our behaviour:

External regulation: eg coercion from other people: "I must"
Introjected regulation: eg avoidance of negative feelings for not doing the behaviour/change: "I should"
Identified regulation: eg acting based on perceived benefits: "I want to"
Integrated regulation: eg doing it because the outcome is important to the self: "It is important to me"

Most clients that hypnotists will see will be coming from one of these standpoints rather than intrinsic. In fact, identified and integrated are likely to be the most beneficial starting points. For example, here are some reasons why smokers may be motivated to quit:

"The doctor tells me I have to" : external
"It's getting to be so socially unacceptable": introjected
"I want to set a good example to the children": identified
"It doesn't fit with anything else in my life anymore": integrated

There may be a small element of intrinsic for some, that is, wanting to achieve the satisfaction of becoming a non-smoker.

Let's look at another typical area: wanting to be free of a flying phobia. Here are some reasons:

Extrinsic Motivation

This is being motivated by factors outside the process itself, such as rewards, approval or pressure.

It can be delineated into a continuum of self-determination:

- **External:** **I must**
- **Introjected:** **I should**
- **Identified:** **I want to**
- **Integrated:** **It is important to me**

"I want to see the world": identified
"My son's getting married in Australia": external
"It is getting in the way of my self-image as a sensible person": integrated
"My wife says that people who fear flying are wimps": introjected

There is more scope in some areas than others to look at intrinsic motivation. For example, encouraging a weight control client to realise that walking can give the intrinsic benefit of being enjoyable, as can healthy eating, might be the key to success.

There is one more element in this structure: this is 'amotivation' (or a lack of motivation), but we will not go into this in detail here. Hypnotists are unlikely to be working with these people, unless in a medical or psychiatric context. For these, the challenge is to generate as much extrinsic (within parameters previously discussed) and intrinsic motivation as you can!

The needs detailed within self-determination theory are also important factors for consideration. If a behaviour or change will help the client feel more competent, related or autonomous (or any combination of these), they are more likely to succeed. Once again these are factors that you can maximise in your interventions.

Canadian psychologist Robert J. Vallerand (1997) organises the constructs of intrinsic and extrinsic motivation into a hierarchical model. Essentially he proposes that intrinsic and extrinsic motivation (and amotivation), feature at global, contextual and situational levels. At each level there are antecedents (such as either global, contextual or situational factors and needs for autonomy, competence and relatedness) as well as affective, cognitive and behavioural consequences.

The global level refers to a general motivational orientation to which people typically subscribe. The contextual level of the model refers to domains of life, such as work, leisure, family. Finally, the situational level is concerned with situation-specific motivation.

For example a client may be a generally highly motivated person, who has strong motivation for maintaining control of his eating habits (general and contextual), but really struggles to maintain this when working on the computer after his family have all gone to bed.

Levels of motivation

Global: typical orientation of motivation for the individual

Contextual: motivation in specific domains, eg work, leisure, family

Situational: the narrowest band, eg an element of a work role

Attribution Theory

Attributions are the perceived causes and reasons that people give for an outcome or behaviour. Weiner (1995) states that the main elements of attribution are ability, effort, task difficulty and luck. Attributions are typically either internal or external. These elements and divisions are related to the consequences of motivation, cognition and emotion.

For example, making attributions to stable factors is likely to lead to expectations that similar results will occur again in the future, whereas unstable attributions provide less clear-cut information about expectations. Similarly, attributions to internal factors are thought to heighten emotional feelings whereas external attributions may lessen emotion.

Subsequently it has been found that the internal/external dimension will affect feelings of self-esteem and pride whereas feelings of controllability relate to such feelings as guilt and pity. For example, successfully quitting smoking, if attributed to planning well for being a non-smoker may result in feelings of pride, whereas failure to quit, if attributed to lack of effort (controllable) may produce feelings of guilt.

Attribution theory

Clients may attribute success or failure to ability, effort, task difficulty or luck.

Attributions can be internal or external, stable or unstable.

A particular element of attribution theory is learned helplessness. This is a challenge for the hypnotist. Learned helplessness can be global, contextual or situational, and is a state that describes the process by which a person has negative experiences and then generalises them to the point where they simply "know" that there is no hope for them. Global learned helplessness may manifest as depression (although depression is not always linked with learned helplessness). Contextual learned helplessness would be, for example, the client who is very successful at work, and can form good working relationships but feels useless at developing personal relationships. An example of a situational learned helplessness may be the schoolboy who is competent in every subject, except maths.

Learned helplessness

Learned helplessness can be global, contextual or situational. It comes about when a client has experienced failure in such a way that they "decide" that there is no point trying anymore as they "just can't do it".

Lewis and Daltroy (1990) have proposed six possible applications of attributional principles to health education. These are equally applicable to the work of the hypnotist, and this list has been adjusted to use terms applicable to this field:

1. Development of therapeutic relationships: eliciting attributions can assist in the development of empathy between hypnotist and client.
2. Creation of correct attributions: assistance in developing informed judgements about one's health status may be important for psychosocial adjustment, particularly where illness is concerned.
3. Alteration of incorrect attributions: attributional change may be functional, either through misattribution alteration or through changes made in the dimensional structure of the attributions formed.
4. Alteration of the focus of the attribution: sometimes the attributional focus may need to be shifted away from one area (for example, uncontrollable illness) to another. This may act as a coping mechanism or assist in personal adjustment.
5. Attribution of characteristics of the individual: hypnotists can use attributional statements in reference to the individual client or patient. These might motivate behaviours if the statements give certain cues to the individual, such as how good a person they are or how capable they are.
6. Maintenance of perceived personal effectiveness: making the right attributions will have an influence on perceived competence and efficacy for the maintenance of their health behaviours.

Competence

The second range of motivation theories are categorised under the heading of competence. These are the "I can!" theories. As previously stated, clear delineation is not possible, but this section will include self-perception, competence and social-cognitive theories.

Social-cognitive theory is essentially "an approach to understanding human cognition, action, motivation and emotion that assumes that people are capable of self-reflection and self-regulation and are active shapers of their environments rather than simply passive reactors to their environments" (Maddux 1993). Maddux outlines five central points to the approach:

- People can symbolise events and have the capacity to anticipate consequences through forethought
- This forethought guides behaviour through goals
- People are self-reflective and this sets the stage for self-control of thought and behaviour
- People can self-regulate through the selection and alteration of environmental conditions
- Events, emotion, cognition and biology are mutually interacting influences

Contemporary self-esteem theory proposes that our global view of ourselves is underpinned by perceptions of specific domains of our lives. Richard Shavelson has suggested that there are four primary domains, academic, social, emotional and physical. All of these can be further subdivided, for example, academic could be split into subject areas, and physical could be split into physical ability and physical appearance.

It is proposed that everyday events are likely to affect more specific perceptions of self and, given time and perhaps effort, may rise up the hierarchy. Short term and trivial experiences are unlikely to affect global self-worth unless specific tactics are utilised to this end.

Shavelson's theory

This theory is that there are four primary domains of self-esteem, all of which can be chunked down (two of many possible examples give for each domain):

- academic
  - maths
  - languages
- social
  - friendships
  - making small talk
- emotional
  - dealing with rejection
  - expressing feelings
- physical
  - sporting ability
  - appearance

Self-perception and Competence Motivation Theory

Harter has delineated various domains of competence perception/adequacy, which become more delineated with age. This framework can be useful for the hypnotist. The theory suggests that people are motivated in achievement domains where their competence can be demonstrated particularly if they are intrinsically motivated and perceive themselves as having an internal locus of control. Successful mastery attempts under such conditions are associated with positive emotion and low anxiety.

In this book we will concentrate on the domains relevant to adults. If you work with children or teenagers (see p180, Special Considerations), you may like to see Harter's ideas for these groups (see p186, Further Reading).

The domains identified are sociability, job competence, nurturance, athletic abilities, physical appearance, adequate provider, morality, household management, intimate relationships, intelligence and sense of humour. When we come to discuss Motivational Hypnotism, we will demonstrate how these domains can effectively be targeted to increase motivation.

Harter's theory

This theory is that there are different domains of competence/adquacy:

- sociability
- job competence
- nurturance
- athletic abilities
- physical appearance
- adequate provider
- morality
- household management
- intimate relationships
- inteliigence
- sense of humour

Goals Perspective Theory

Maehr & Nicholls (1980) defined three types of achievement motivation: ability-orientated motivation, task-orientated motivation and social approval-orientated motivation. Ability-orientated motivation is when 'the goal of the behavior is to maximize the subjective probability of attributing high ability to oneself' (Maehr and Nicholls 1980). Sometimes this is referred to as ego-orientation.

In task-orientation motivation, according to Maehr and Nicholls (1980), 'the primary goal is to produce an adequate product or to solve a problem for its own sake rather than to demonstrate ability'. The third goal, social approval-orientated motivation is defined in terms of demonstration of conformity to norms or virtuous intent.

The first two are dependent on how people construe competence. In task-orientation cues are effort and task completion and hence self-referenced but with ego-orientation competence is usually judged relative to others and ability and effort are differentiated as causes of outcomes. This is an externally referenced view. The orientation affects not only attitude to goals, but also the nature of the goals that are set.

It is useful to understand the relationship between an individual's goal orientation and their intrinsic/extrinsic motivational constructs, and their perception of ability, and its relative necessity. Underlying belief structures and goal behaviour will be affected by and will affect situational achievement. Also, task and ego orientation are not mutually exclusive. An individual may be generally high in one and low in the other, or high in both or low in both. Similarly with contextual or situational motivation any combination is possible, and variable.

Research has shown that high task orientation is positive, whether combined with high ego-orientation or not. Studies have been undertaken to discover where orientation is developed, but for our purposes this is of less interest than knowing how to ascertain what orientations are, and how to work with these to increase motivation.

Goal perspectives

Task orientation is where the client considers effort and where completion is the aim. It tends to be self-referenced.

Ego orientation is where the client considers ability and effort and the outcome is usually judged relative to others.

Self-efficacy Theory

Confidence has been identified at the anecdotal and empirical level as an important construct in motivation. There is an assumption that behavioural outcomes influence self-efficacy and onwards to self-esteem. This reflects a 'psychological consequences' approach to self-efficacy. However, self-efficacy theory also supports the reciprocal nature of the relationship between efficacy perceptions and behaviour by stating that the behaviour will not be indulged in unless efficacy perceptions are sufficient. This is dealing with the motivational role of self-efficacy and will be the approach adopted here.

Bandura (1986) defines self-efficacy as:

"People's judgement of their capabilities to organise and execute courses of action required to attain designated types of performances. It is concerned not with the skills one has but with judgements of what one can do with whatever skills one possesses."

He differentiates between the beliefs related to the ability to carry out a particular behaviour (efficacy expectations) and beliefs as to whether the behaviour will produce a particular result (outcome expectations). For example, efficacy expectations may be the belief that one can successfully adhere to a programme of brisk walking five times a week for thirty minutes each. However, outcome expectations may refer to whether one believes that such activity will produce the weight loss that was desired when planning the activity.

There are four main sources of information for efficacy beliefs according to Bandura:

1. Prior success and performance attainment

This is thought to be the most powerful, since it is based on personal experience, but appraisal of such events is likely to influence expectations of future success. Attribution theory predicts that internal and stable causes of failure (such as lack of ability) are more likely to lead to debilitating and demotivating cognitions and negative emotions than factors which appear more changeable (such as lack of effort).

Attributional factors may also be important in determining the extent that efficacy expectations gained in one context generalise to other contexts. Bandura (1986) suggests that some generalisation is likely and is predicted to be strongest in similar events to the original source of efficacy judgements.

This is useful for the hypnotist, as it opens up the opportunity for generalising past successes on to the present challenge, and also allowing and encouraging development of progress through taking small steps towards a goal.

2. Imitation and modelling

Observing others succeed or fail could affect subsequent efficacy beliefs, particularly if the individual has little or no prior experience to draw on. In the setting of the work of the hypnotist, this can most clearly be seen in the use of surface structure metaphors, but is also often the case where clients self-refer following the success of a friend.

3. Verbal and social persuasion

Depending on the source of such self-efficacy information, persuasion from others is likely to influence perceptions of self-efficacy. However, it is thought to be a relatively weak source in comparison to the two already mentioned. The success of persuasion is also dependent on the realistic nature of the information.

The hypnotist has a role to play here. You can be the client's champion in their efforts to succeed, encouraging and supporting their efforts and self-efficacy.

4. Judgements of physiological states

The original theorising on SET was based on modifications of reactions to aversive events such as phobias (Bandura 1977). In such situations it was found that self-efficacy was related to how one appraised internal physiological states such as heart rate.

The hypnotist's role here is to help the client become aware of differences. You are in a unique position to do this, especially as the process of inducing hypnosis will in itself produce changes.

Self efficacy theory

This theory is that people judge their capabilities to organise and execute courses of action required to attain designated types of performances. It is concerned not with the skills one has but with judgements of what one can do with whatever skills one possesses. It covers both judgement of

- **belief in ability, and**
- **belief that the action will result in the outcome**

The following are the factors defined as being the basis of self-efficacy:

- **prior success**
- **imitation and modelling**
- **verbal and social persuasion**
- **judgements of physiological states**

Beliefs

A client's beliefs and attitudes will always be a major factor in their motivation to change. Health promotion programmes often concentrate highly on this area, but research suggests that changing attitudes is not sufficient for behaviour change to be made although it is a useful starting point.

There is no universally accepted definition of attitude, although a well-established model (Hovland and Rosenberg (1960)) suggests that attitudes have three elements: beliefs (cognitive), affective (emotional) and behavioural. Attitude, like personality and motivation is hypothetical and not open to direct observation. Hypnotists will, for the most part, be interpreting verbal and non-verbal cues in each of these categories.

The Theory of Reasoned Action

This theory, proposed by Ajzen and Fishbein (1980) is concerned with the antecedents of volitional behaviour. It is based on the assumption that intention is an immediate determinant of behaviour and that intention, in turn, is predicted from attitude and subjective normative factors. These subjective normative factors are comprised of the beliefs of significant others and the extent that one wishes or is motivated to comply with such beliefs or people.

The relative importance of attitudinal and normative components will depend on the situation under investigation. For example, it may be supposed that the attitudinal component would be more important for a middle-aged client wanting to improve her golf handicap and the normative more important for a teenaged client who wished to play better football.

There are some problems with the TRA model. It is unidirectional and fails to consider environmental issues, it predicts behaviour from the intention at a fixed point in time and does not take previous behaviour (eg habit) into consideration. A revised theory is explained below.

Theory of reasoned action

This theory states that behaviour is determined by intention, and that intention is determined by attitude and subjective norms.

The theory is uni-directional and does not take into account the environment. It predicts behaviour from intention at a fixed point and excludes previous behaviours (eg habits)

The Theory of Planned Behaviour

The TRA model has proved successful in predicting behaviour and intentions for actions that are primarily volitional and controllable. However there are many behaviours where volitional control is incomplete. Ajzen has proposed an addition to the TRA (creating the TPB), that is the variable 'perceived behaviour control'. This is defined by Ajzen (1988) as 'the perceived ease or difficulty of performing the behaviour' and is assumed to reflect past experience as well as anticipated impediments and obstacles. The TPB is a very popular model in health psychology today.

In the world of hypnotism the extra factor is very important. It is also critical to recognise that perceived behavioural control will accurately predict behaviour only under circumstances when perceived control closely approximates actual control. This is a key area for our work.

Theory of planned behaviour

This theory adds "perceived behaviour control" to the previous theory.

This perception will reflect previous experience and anticipated obstacles.

Triandis' Theory of Social Behaviour

Triandis (1977) proposed an attitude model that has some similarities with the TRA and TPB although stresses less conscious decision-making at some points in the model. The model specifies that the likelihood of acting out a particular behaviour will be dependent on:

- Prior behaviour ('habit')
- Behavioural intention
- Facilitating conditions

Triandis suggests that as the strength of the habit increases, so the level of volition decreases which makes this strength an important factor. This has two distinct uses, firstly awareness of this factor will help in our work with clients who have unwanted habits, and secondly it will assist us working with clients for whom new beneficial habits need to be installed.

This model is rarely used, but is included here due to the inclusion of the habit factor: often critical in the work of the hypnotist.

Theory of social behaviour

This theory includes the following factors:

- **Prior behaviour ('habit')**
- **Behavioural intention**
- **Facilitating conditions**

It is rarely used, but is significant for hypnotists in that it recognises strength of habit and its link to level of volition.

The Health Belief Model

This model was developed to help explain health behaviours. However there are elements that can be generalised to other areas of a hypnotist's work. It was developed from Kurt Lewin's 'field theory', a phenomenological approach which advocated that behaviour is influenced by the individual's characteristics and environment.

The theory states that we live in a 'life space' of regions of both positive and negative value and forces attract and repel us from these. Illness is a region of negative value and hence we are motivated to avoid it most of the time and this forms a central tenet of the HBM.

Rosenstock (1990) states that 'for more than three decades, the model has been one of the most influential and widely used psychosocial approaches to explaining health-related behaviour'. The model hypothesises that people will not seek (preventive) health measures unless:

- They possess minimal levels of health motivation and knowledge
- They view themselves as potentially vulnerable
- They view the condition as threatening
- They are convinced of the efficacy of the 'treatment'
- They see few difficulties in undertaking the action

These factors can be modified by socio-economic and demographic factors as well as cues to action such as media campaigns or the illness of a close friend or relative.

Health belief model

This is a model of human behaviour with regard to avoiding illness. It states that people will only seek preventative measures is they have knowledge of the illnesses, feel vulnerable, feel that the condition is threatening, believe the measures will work and that it will not be difficult.

Hypnotists can extend this model for issues other than illness, ie avoidance of anything potentially negative.

Reviewing the literature in 1984, Janz and Becker claim that:

- The model has substantial support following extensive research
- 'Perceived barriers' was the most consistently powerful predictor

- Beliefs associated with susceptibility are more important in preventive health behaviours
- Beliefs in the perceived benefits of action are more important in illness behaviours

Not all research has proved so conclusive. As with other models the critical process for hypnotists is to take the ideas and consider them when working with individual clients.

Protection Motivation Theory

Rogers (1983) proposed a model that has similarities with the TRA/TPB and HBM. His 'protection motivation theory' is a cognitive model based on expectancy-value principles and was originally developed as an explanation for the effects of 'fear appeals' in health behaviour change. It is a model of health decision-making wherein intentions are predicted from the following factors:

- Perceived severity
- Perceived probability
- Efficacy of preventive behaviour
- Perceived self-efficacy

From these, the individual has appraised the threat and coping strategy that may lead to an intention to protect, and if it does, the model states that this leads to protective behaviour.

The key area here for the hypnotist to address is the last one: perceived self-efficacy. It is necessary to take care with the other elements. Let's take smoking cessation as an example, and the threat of lung cancer as the motivator. The client will have a perception of the severity and probability. The hypnotist may have statistics that can be passed on, but these must be as accurate and objective as possible, or the hypnotist could risk inflating this side of the scales, that is encouraging a belief that the risk is too great to be addressed. Likewise, exaggerating the efficacy of a preventive behaviour can be damaging as it may lead to an inappropriate reliance. For example, if a client has a serious illness, exaggerating the effectiveness of hypnotism may lead to them ignoring conventional medicine to their detriment.

This model has a particular limitation. Godin (1994) states: "in general, messages conveying a persuasive threat seem effective in enhancing participants' intention to change their behaviours, but they are less effective in inducing and sustaining changes in behavior."

Protection motivation theory

This is a model to be used with care: it uses the variables severity, probability, efficacy of behaviour and self-efficacy to predict behaviour.

Hypnotists can maximise self-efficacy, and work with the other variables in some cases.

(Further details in full text).

Entity and incremental views

Dweck (1992) has differentiated between two clusters of beliefs that underpin people's judgements and actions. Those that subscribe to the view that a particular attribute is fixed and relatively stable hold an 'entity' view and those that see the attribute as changeable and open to development hold an 'incremental' view.

Those who hold an entity view are more likely to have negative reactions, such as helplessness, when faced with achievement setbacks. Those with entity views are more likely to set ego goals, and those with incremental views are more likely to set task goals.

This theory is useful in building awareness. Few clients will be aware, when they arrive at the hypnotist's office, whether they have an entity or incremental view! Nor will they be aware of their underlying processes, but by discovering this, you may be able to assist the client to find a way of being that is most beneficial for their circumstances.

Entity and incremental views

Entity view: belief that attributes (eg ability) is relatively fixed

Incremental view: belief that attributes are open to development

Decision-making

In this section we will concentrate on just one theory. As you will have gathered, many of the models in other categories involve decision-making, but the Transtheoretical model has received much attention by researchers over recent years.

Transtheoretical Model of Behaviour Change

The TTM was developed as a comprehensive model of behaviour change and was initially applied to smoking cessation (Prochaska and DiClemente 1983). It incorporates cognitive, behavioural and temporal aspects of changing behaviour. The TTM consists of the stages of change, the processes of change, decisional balance and self-efficacy. The stage of change is the time dimension along which behaviour change occurs (the 'when'), and the other elements are the 'how' and 'why'. The stages are:

- Precontemplation- no intention of change
- Contemplation - intention to make a change, usually within 6 months
- Preparation - immediate intention (within 30 days) and commitment to change (sometimes accompanied by small behavioural changes in preparation)
- Action - making the change.
- Maintenance- maintaining the change long term.

It is important that the change is clearly defined and concise. Many people have relapses when attempting behaviour change and methods for coping with this should be built into all interventions. Learning from failure can be a beneficial process for long term success.

Stages of change

- Precontemplation
- Contemplation
- Preparation
- Action
- Maintenance

The processes of change are the strategies used to progress along the stages of change. The processes are divided into experiential (where information is gathered through experiences) and behavioural (where information is gathered through the environment and actions. The experiential processes are more important in the early stages and behavioural more important later.

These processes can be subdivided:

Experiential (thinking) processes

1. Consciousness raising- seeking new information
2. Dramatic relief - experiencing and expressing intense feelings and emotions about NOT making the change
3. Environmental re-evaluation - assessing how the change will affect physical and social environments
4. Self re-evaluation - cognitive and emotional reappraisal of values
5. Social liberation - developing an awareness and acceptance of new lifestyle

Thinking processes of change

- Consciousness raising
- Dramatic relief
- Environmental re-evaluation
- Self re-evaluation
- Social liberation

Behavioural (doing) processes

1. Counter-conditioning - substitute alternatives for current behaviour
2. Helping relationships - use support from others to make and sustain change
3. Reinforcement management - change contingencies and reward new behaviours
4. Self liberation - choose and commit to change, believe that one can change
5. Stimulus control - control situations and cues that interfere with new behaviours

Doing processes of change

- Counter-conditioning
- Helping relationships
- Reinforcement management
- Self-liberation
- Stimulus control

Decisional balance is the evaluation of the costs and benefits (or pros and cons) of engaging in a behaviour or making a change. Each consists of four categories:

- Approval and instrumental gains by self
- Approval and instrumental gains by others
- Disapproval and losses by self
- Disapproval and losses by others

Self-efficacy is also a factor of the TTM and has been found to increase, linearly, through the stages.

Theories of hypnotism

Introduction

This chapter gives an outline of the three most common ways that hypnotism is taught and practised. It is important to note that many hypnotists use a combination of two or three modes, and we strongly believe that all have their place. It is our opinion that an eclectic, congruent approach to hypnotism is the most effective way. For example, we know of hypnotists who use an analytical approach for every client, or others who never do. This seems to us to be unnecessarily limiting, and in this chapter we will discuss some of the pros and cons of choosing each method for different presenting issues.

Analytical

There are various methods within the Analytical family of hypnotic techniques. They all involve age regression, achieved by a variety of tools. These include:

- Time line
- Free association
- Affect bridge

They also have in common the fact that they are regressing in order to find the root cause of a current situation. Some theories state that the root cause will always be a memory or emotion that is repressed. However, there is dissension within the profession as to what repression really means, or even if it is a real process at all. Heap and Aravind (2002) include an excellent discussion on the concept of repressed memories, so we shall not recreate their ideas here, but point you in this direction if you are interested to read further.

Hypno-Analysis is a combination of the principles of hypnotism and traditional forms of psychoanalysis from the schools of Freud, Jung, Adler, and Kein.

By going back through the client's history, usually to the age of seven or earlier (imprinting phase of development) the hypnotist and client can look effectively at the genuine cause of their issue. Before the age of 7 children generally cannot see the world other than in a "black and white" or "good or bad" way. The client at this age does not have the ability to see the psychological maturity to see situations other than in this form, whilst as we grow older we learn that situations often fit into a shade of grey, neither completely good nor bad.

When the client is at this age they made certain decisions which at an unconscious level effect the life of the client in the present. This decision is carried out through the client's life. Often the issue does not have an obvious direct link with the root cause, but through analysis of thoughts ideas and beliefs the hypnotist and client can come to certain understandings in order to assist the client in moving forward.

Using regression to help the client to rationalise the root cause of the client using the client's "adult mind", allows the client to leave the past in the past and move forward with a new sense of calm and peace. This rationalisation can take the form of simple understanding or emotional catharsis.

Analytical processes vary in the degree to which abreaction is encouraged or even required for resolution to be found. Some schools of thought insist that reliving traumatic events is necessary to progress while others say that "watching" events from a dissociated viewpoint is sufficient to bring about the necessary awareness.

Often the key that is being sought in Analytical work is the so-called "Aha! moment". Often it is considered that once this has been found, the client will have understanding of the reason for their issue, and thus it will be resolved. Others believe that this memory or realisation or new awareness needs to be worked on in order to produce resolution.

In our opinion, age regression can be a very useful technique to employ for clients with certain issues, such as phobia, anxiety, certain medical issues, and for those who have a belief that there are lessons to be learnt. We do not however, believe that this is the way to go for every client and with every issue. For example, when a client presents wanting to stop smoking, we have found it to be rare that there is a need to regress to find why they started to smoke. It is usually exceptionally obvious to the client.

Ericksonian

One of the key figures in the history of hypnotism was Milton H Erickson. His approach is often described as indirect, but if you watch videos of him in action you will see that he could be very direct. He used a combination of suggestion and metaphor to produce unconscious understanding, and hence the opportunity for the client to choose to change.

The advantage of the Ericksonian model of hypnotism is that it is more dependent on the client's experience rather than the suggestions of the hypnotist. This allows for the client to drive the process based on what exactly they wants. Unfortunately, if a client is not particularly clear on their outcomes, Ericksonian hypnotism can be frustrating for the client who might need more direction.

Ericksonian work is based principally around four key components:

a. Utilisation
b. Milton Model Linguistic Patterns
c. Metaphor
d. Fractionalisation

Utilisation is the harnessing of whatever the client brings into the hypnotic session to assist them in achieving the stated outcomes. This differs from approaches which can be more dismissive of the factors that a client brings into the hypnotic session.

The Milton Model Linguistic Patterns are 19 specifically determined patterns discovered by Bandler and Grinder, whilst doing early research for the Neuro Linguistic Programming process. These patterns are designed to get the client to search their own unconscious for solutions and answers.

Metaphor is the use of stories and analogies to act as a bridge for the client from where they are now to where they want to be. Hypnotists can utilise either deep structure or surface structure metaphors for this purpose. Deep structure metaphors are stories where the meaning is not obvious in the context of the story, while surface structure metaphors are where the meaning of the story is obvious.

Fractionalisation is the use of the induction of trance several times within the session in order to deepen the experience. Usually a hypnotist will instruct a client to open their eyes at various parts of the session, without formally reviving the client in order to then ask them to close them again and to go even deeper into trance.

Cognitive / behavioural

Cognitive Behavioural Therapy is a form of treatment which requires clients to look at the importance of thinking in what they feel and what they do. Traditionally this treatment involves the identification of negative thoughts and how they effect the client's behaviour. Once this is done then strategies are looked at as to how overcome these thoughts for a more constructive way of thinking and living.

Cognitive Behavioural Therapy theory is that thoughts mediate between stimuli (eg. external events and emotions). In this approach and theory, it is not emotion which causes a direct emotional response but it is the evaluation of the emotion which causes the response. The therapy itself is designed to help the client to become more aware of distorted thoughts and how these thoughts cause psychological distress. It also looks at the behavioural patterns of the client which reinforce the distress. The outcome is not to correct every distorted outlook. As NLP Practitioners know, distortion is one of the three primary filters which information must go through to be processed. Rather it is the goal of CBT to get the client to understand these distortions in order to make effective behavioural change. Much of the therapeutic intervention occurs between sessions in the form of tasks the client is set to carry out in order to help their own recovery process.

This approach fits well to hypnotism in that when we work with clients it is possible to utilise the formal trance state in order to determine the roots of our client's thoughts and once this is done a hypnotist can then assist the client in making changes in their thoughts through the use of hypnosis. Once this change in thought occurs it is far more likely that the client's attitudes and beliefs will be changed. Change the attitudes and beliefs and you change the behaviour, even when this is not specifically discussed.

There is much research which has shown that Cognitive Behavioural Therapy efficacy is increased when hypnotism is employed as part of the treatment. There is also much research into the use of hypnotism and CBT in the treatment of anxiety disorders, hypertension, the relief of pain, IBS, phobias, OCD's, tension and stress. It should be noted that with most of these interventions, the use of self hypnosis appears to help make the treatment more effective.

Motivational Hypnotism

We now come to the section of the book where we can introduce the Motivational Model of Hypnotism. All of the previous sections have been used to formulate this model, and it is very much a working model, one that can be adapted to most situations and that will develop in the future. It is also a model that is adaptable to an individual's own style. Being yourself when in the role of hypnotist is one of the most crucial factors for success, so we encourage you to use this model in the way that suits you and your clients.

In this section we will go through the basic model in two parts, firstly information gathering, and secondly, hypnotic intervention. The first is used to prepare your strategy for the second. In the practical chapters that follow, we will show you how to use the model for different issues, and how different elements of the model have more importance at times than others. Here you will see the need to be flexible, and with flexibility comes a personal approach that ensures your clients are treated as individuals.

Information Gathering

Here follows a list of the elements of motivation that may be relevant for you to ascertain in your initial session with your client.

GOAL

- direction - is movement required towards something or away from something?
- value - how important is meeting the goal? does it fit with the client's value system?
- difficulty - how hard does the client feel it will be to achieve?
- identity - is the client's identity integral to behaviour as is, or as will be?
- barriers - what obstacles are perceived by the client, and do you see any others that they have missed?
- orientation - is this goal primarily ego or task orientated?
- support - does the client have support in making this change?
- SMART - is the goal
  Specific ?
  Measurable ?
  Adjustable?
  Realistic?
  Time-based?

CONTROL

- where is the client's typical Locus of Control?
- specifically for this goal, where is their Locus of Control?
- how much control do they perceive they have over their behaviour and the outcome of that behaviour?
- how realistic do you feel their perceptions to be?

INTRINSIC MOTIVATION

How much of the following would the process of reaching the goal bring the client?

- ☐ feeling of making a free choice
- ☐ interest
- ☐ challenge
- ☐ enjoyment

How much would the process of reaching the goal, and the end result help meet the following needs?

- ☐ relatedness
- ☐ competence
- ☐ autonomy

EXTRINSIC MOTIVATION

How much does the client agree with these statements?

- ☐ I must do it
- ☐ I should do it
- ☐ I want to do it
- ☐ It is important to me to do it

GENERAL MOTIVATION

How high does the client rate their own motivation?

- ☐ Globally
- ☐ Contextually
- ☐ Situationally

Give guidance by providing examples

ATTRIBUTIONS

- ☐ does the client generally attribute success to internal or external factors?
- ☐ does the client generally attribute failure to internal or external factors?
- ☐ if the client has previously failed to reach this goal, do they attribute this to internal or external factors?
- ☐ are there any signs of learned helplessness, generally or specifically to this goal?

SELF-PERCEPTION

- ☐ confidence - how confident is the client generally? How confident are they in the behaviours necessary to reach the goal?
- ☐ ability - do they tend towards an entity or incremental view? Do they believe they are capable of reaching the goal?
- ☐ outcome - do they believe that the planned behaviour will result in reaching the goal?
- ☐ success - do they have prior successes in similar areas they can draw from?
- ☐ imitation - do they know of anyone who has achieved the goal? Do you?
- ☐ worthiness - do they feel they deserve to reach the goal?
- ☐ persuasion - is there anyone persuading them to reach the goal? If so, do they perceive this as helpful or not?

(NB in the practical chapters, we will utilise both the models of Shavelson and Harter specifically for the issue in question to add to this information)

ATTITUDE

- ☐ beliefs - how does meeting the goal fit the client's belief system?
- ☐ emotions - what emotions are linked to both success and failure in reaching the goal?
- ☐ behaviour - how does the client's current behaviour assist or hinder the process of reaching the goal?
- ☐ others - do others have an influence on the process of reaching the goal?
- ☐ habit - if a habit is to be broken, how strong does the client perceive it to be? Do they have a tendency towards being habitual?

PHYSIOLOGY

- ☐ what physical feelings are associated with both the client's current position and the intended position on reaching the goal?

- ☐ does the client have sufficient knowledge of the physiological processes involved?

ENVIRONMENT

- ☐ in what ways may the client's physical and social environment affect the process of moving towards their goal?
- ☐ when the goal is reached, will there be any conflict with their physical or social environment?

PROs and CONs

Assist the client to draw up a list of all the pros and cons of achieving the goal. For each, ascertain:

- the perceived severity (how good or bad it will be)
- the perceived probability of this happening
- how much effect the behaviour is likely to have to increase/reduce (as appropriate), the severity and/or likelihood of the outcome

Examine:

- approval and gains for the client
- approval and gains for others
- disapproval and losses for self
- disapproval and losses for others

In addition to this information, you will still, of course, need to ask all the usual questions so that you have a good all round picture of the client that you are working with.

Intervention

You will now have a lot of motivational information on which to base your intervention and it is now time for you to plan your strategy. The strategy will vary depending on the issue you are working with, the information you have gathered, your preferred working style, your previous experience and the client's wishes.

Please note that this model can be combined with any other way of working, but for ease of explanation we will presume here that it is being used as a stand-alone model.

ELEMENTS for INTERVENTION STRATEGIES

Select and use in whatever order is appropriate:

- ☐ guide the client through a guided imagery to experience intensely the emotions associated with achieving and/or not achieving the goal
- ☐ build an awareness and acceptance of how things will be, both en route, and when the goal is achieved
- ☐ suggest (following discussion) substitutes for current behaviour, where appropriate (some behaviours will not need substitutes)
- ☐ move the client further towards the 'integrated' end of the extrinsic continuum
- ☐ maximise intrinsic motivation
- ☐ suggest self-rewards if appropriate
- ☐ strengthen beliefs
- ☐ highlight the ways that the goal fits the client's value system
- ☐ suggest (following discussions) ways to control stimuli
- ☐ work with pros and cons; presuming the client does want to go ahead, enhance pros, and minimise cons.
- ☐ if possible create awareness of a goal as being toward positivity and away from negativity
- ☐ maximise the client's belief in their ability to succeed
- ☐ maximise task orientation (when appropriate)
- ☐ tie client's identity in with end result and separate from current behaviour
- ☐ help the client to find ways over, under, around or through barriers, or to remove or reduce them
- ☐ assist the client in maximising their environment and support
- ☐ use ego-strengthening techniques and build on past successes
- ☐ boost feeling of control, and help them to have more in reality
- ☐ if motivation is high in other contexts, transfer it
- ☐ reduce perception of the strength of the habit
- ☐ assist the client towards internal attributions
- ☐ educate the client as to physiological processes
- ☐ address perceived competence/adequacy using the Harter model
- ☐ address self-esteem using the Shavelson model
- ☐ assist client to be aware of possible set-backs and how to deal with them

Practical applications

Smoking cessation

GOAL: non-smoking

There is a simple goal here that is well-defined: to quit smoking. Occasionally a client will want to cut down, but this is still a clear goal.

- ☐ direction - a client is likely to be moving away from negative health consequences, and social issues, and/or towards better health, acceptance etc. Both can be maximised
- ☐ value - how important is it for this client to stop smoking? In what ways does it fit, or not, their value system? How can you use this in your intervention?
- ☐ difficulty - how hard does the client feel it will be to become a non-smoker?
- ☐ identity - is the client's identity integral to being a smoker? How can you help them see themselves as a non-smoker ?
- ☐ barriers - what obstacles are perceived by the client, and do you see any others that they have missed?
- ☐ support - does the client have support in becoming a non-smoker?
- ☐ SMART - the goal is specific, measurable, realistic (for most, and this will become apparent), and time-based (they are stopping at a defined point). It is not an adjustable goal, however, but we wouldn't want to build that in for the sake of it!

CONTROL: non-smoking

- ☐ where is the client's typical Locus of Control?
- ☐ specifically for this goal, where is their Locus of Control?
- ☐ how much control do they perceive they have over their smoking?
- ☐ how much do they feel that smoking is a habit or an addiction? Usually, the more towards the habit end of the continuum they are, the better
- ☐ how realistic do you feel their perceptions to be? Do you need to work with these?

INTRINSIC MOTIVATION: non-smoking

By becoming a non-smoker, the client is likely to:

- ☐ get a feeling of making a free choice
- ☐ not find the process interesting
- ☐ perceive it as a challenge
- ☐ not expect it to be enjoyable (so emphasise the enjoyable elements of being a non-smoker)

Becoming a non-smoker can help the client

- ☐ feel more related- less of a social outcast
- ☐ feel competent: they are achieving something important
- ☐ gain autonomy: tobacco is no longer controlling them

EXTRINSIC MOTIVATION: non-smoking

How much does the client agree with these statements?

- ☐ I must stop smoking
- ☐ I should stop smoking
- ☐ I want to stop smoking
- ☐ It is important to me to be a non-smoker

ATTRIBUTIONS: non-smoking

- ☐ does the client generally attribute success to internal or external factors?
- ☐ does the client generally attribute failure to internal or external factors?
- ☐ if the client has previously failed to stop smoking, do they attribute this to internal or external factors?
- ☐ are there any signs of learned helplessness, generally or specifically to stopping smoking?

GENERAL MOTIVATION: non-smoking

How high does the client rate their own motivation?

- ☐ Globally
- ☐ Contextually
- ☐ Situationally

Give guidance by providing examples

SELF-PERCEPTION: non-smoking

- ☐ confidence - how confident is the client generally?
- ☐ ability - do they tend towards an entity or incremental view? Do they believe they are capable of becoming a non-smoker?
- ☐ outcome - using the reasons they have stated for wanting to stop, how strongly do they believe that stopping will produce the desired result? Eg, if they want to stop to avoid cancer, do they truly believe that this will work?
- ☐ success - do they have prior successes in similar areas they can draw from? Maybe giving up other habits, or controlling their eating?
- ☐ imitation - do they know of anyone who has achieved the goal? You can use surface structure metaphor here.
- ☐ worthiness - do they feel they deserve the outcome they are looking for (eg health or belonging) ?
- ☐ persuasion - is there anyone persuading them to reach the goal? If so, do they perceive this as helpful or not?
- ☐ Shavelson - chunk down the Social domain of self-perception to find areas where the client feels particularly confident, or the opposite. Do the same with the Emotional domain. This will give you the information you need to be specific in terms of encouraging their self-confidence
- ☐ Harter - look at the client's perception of competence or adequacy on the following: Sociability, nurturance, Appearance, Provider, Intimate Relationships. More information on which to build

ATTITUDE: non-smoking

- beliefs - how does becoming a non-smoker fit the client's belief system?
- emotions - what emotions are linked to both success and failure in stopping smoking?
- behaviour - how do other behaviours assist or hinder the process, eg exercise, socialising?
- others - do others have an influence on the process of becoming and remaining a non-smoker, eg other smokers in the house?
- habit - How strong does the client perceive the habit/addiction to be? Do they have a tendency towards being habitual?

PHYSIOLOGY: non-smoking

- what physical feelings are associated with both smoking and not smoking?

- does the client have sufficient knowledge of the physiological processes involved?

ENVIRONMENT: non-smoking

- in what ways may the client's physical and social environment affect the process of becoming and remaining a non-smoker?
- when they become a non-smoker, will there be any conflict with their physical or social environment?

PROs and CONs: smoking

Assist the client to draw up a list of all the pros and cons of becoming and remaining a non-smoker. For each, ascertain:

- the perceived severity (how good or bad it will be)
- the perceived probability of this happening
- how much effect giving up smoking is likely to have to increase/reduce (as appropriate), the severity and/or likelihood of the outcome

Examine:

- approval and gains for the client
- approval and gains for others
- disapproval and losses for self
- disapproval and losses for others

Case example: non-smoking

James is a 60 year old factory worker who presented for smoking cessation. The information gathering process elicited the following significant points:

GOAL:

Direction: James is keen to move towards better health so that he can play football with his grandchildren, and away from the "stigmatisation" that he feels is now happening to smokers.

Value: he does not feel that it is very important to be a non-smoker, but likewise, remaining one doesn't hold value either. He has said that he thought he would feel better if he "gave it a go" as his daughter had stopped through hypnosis.

Difficulty: he does not know how difficult it would be. It has been impossible before, but his daughter has found this easy.

Identity: James had started smoking at 15, so his identity could have been highly integrated but he states that he has no problem imagining himself as a non-smoker.

Barriers: James feels that going to the pub will be the biggest problem in becoming a non-smoker. How can he have a pint without a cigarette in his hand?

Support: he has solid support from all his family although his friends at the pub apparently "know he could never do it".

CONTROL:

Locus of control: James has spent 43 years working on the shop floor of a plastics company and has only had any responsibility for others in the last five years when he became foreman. It is clear that he is used to following instruction and not taking responsibility. This is mirrored in his family life which is organised predominantly by his wife. The only area where James feels control over the outcome is his hobby of pigeon racing in which he has had much success.

Specifically: James is aware that no one else can determine whether he smokes or not.

Habit/addiction: he is of the belief that nicotine is addictive, but also aware that there is a habit (half way along the continuum). I feel his perceptions are honest and he has good awareness. I can utilise the pigeon hobby to show his abilities to make determinations for himself.

INTRINSIC MOTIVATION:

James perceives that to become a non-smoker will be a challenge and that it will help him feel more related. He does not expect the process to be enjoyable but he thinks that the end result of being a non-smoker will be. He has not thought of the fact that it could help him to feel competent.

EXTRINSIC MOTIVATION:

James chose the third option, the Identified level.

GENERAL MOTIVATION:

Global: low

Contextual: high for pigeon racing, low for work, recent problems with breathing show his motivation to be able to play with the grandchildren is high.

Situational: medium

ATTRIBUTIONS:

The only successes mentioned were to do with pigeon racing and there attributions were internal (strongly so). Failures, such as not getting promotion earlier, were also attributed internally as were previous attempts to stop smoking. There were signs of learned helplessness in work, but they did not appear to be connected to this habit.

SELF-PERCEPTION:

Confidence: generally not an issue. "Not high, not low, just is!"

Ability: Entity for academic skills, incremental on "doing", eg learning DIY tasks

Outcome: James strongly believes that stopping smoking will give him the outcomes he seeks, and quickly too!

Success: James could not think of other habits he had stopped but he feels in control of his output at the factory and is proud of always meeting targets

Imitation: his daughter has recently quit and a work colleague who was a "hardened smoker" did so a year ago to everyone's surprise

Worthiness: he feels completely worthy of his intended outcomes

Persuasion: his daughter and his grandchildren are pushing him a little but he sees this as positive. He feels "warm" that they care enough to want him around.

Shavelson: James feels particularly confident with his colleagues while at work and with a particular group of three friends at the pub. He lacks confidence when with family members at restaurants and at formal events in his pigeon racing community (both of these are affected by his smoking). Emotionally, James is ok with most emotions although he demonstrated the typical British attitude of the necessity of keeping emotions to oneself. He says that he was "not particularly good" with women who cry.

Harter:

- Sociability: better than adequate
- Nurturance: competent
- Appearance: James feels this was not relevant at 60! He doesn't care anymore
- Provider: adequate
- Intimate relationships: more concerned with relationship with grandchildren than others. He wants them to respect him

ATTITUDE:

Beliefs: being a non-smoker fits well into his belief system of needing to be healthy as an older adult. He values his family highly.

Emotions: James has difficulty expressing his thoughts on emotions, but feels that being a non-smoker will make him feel happy and proud and if he fails he will be disappointed with himself.

Behaviour: other behaviours seem to be quite separate to his smoking habit, except for drinking in the pub and after a meal. In terms of the latter he suggested that he would have a cup of tea instead as his wife does. He also avoids smoking at work even at break time so this is a useful behaviour.

Others: James' friends at the pub are the only ones likely to be able to have a negative influence on his remaining a non-smoker.

Habit: he feels that this was the only negative habit that he can remember having.

PHYSIOLOGY:

Physical feelings: James feels breathless whenever he exerts himself, but feels that smoking relieved this. He believes smoking relaxes him and makes him feel calmer. He feels that when he stops he will feel physical withdrawal symptoms for about three weeks but will then start to feel better than he had before ("clearer").

Knowledge: James did not know very much about the physical processes of smoking or quitting.

ENVIRONMENT:

Home seems as though it will be supportive and enabling, work will be neutral, but the pub could cause problems. This is where the conflict might occur.

PROS:

- Better health: very good and very likely
- Social acceptability: good and very likely
- More money: good and certain
- Good feelings: good and possible
- Respect from grandchildren: very good and likely

CONS:

- Withdrawal: bad or very bad and very likely
- Weight gain: slightly bad and possible
- Irritability: bad and likely

The approval for himself would come from himself and his grandchildren. The gains for himself would be health, money and respect. For others the gains would be to have him around healthier and longer and losses are none. For himself, losses are temporary, and there was a possibility of disapproval from his friends at the pub.

INTERVENTION:

This information was used to create the following suggestions (please note we are not giving the specific wording so as not to unduly influence you. Each hypnotist needs to complete this process in their own style):

- Guided imagery of James feeling happy and proud as a non-smoker playing with his grandchildren, in the pub with his friends (who are surprised!), in a restaurant with his family and at a pigeon event. Also include physical feelings with comments on speed of getting over the nicotine and how much more relaxed he will feel when the stimulant is out of his system.

- To have a cup of tea with his wife after a meal, but otherwise can continue to do all that he used to do just as he did it without the little white stick. No need to substitute anything.

- Use phrase "it is important to you" to move him from identified to integrated intrinsic motivation level.

- Discuss relatedness that will be gained, feelings of achievement, challenge (but do-able, liken to pigeon racing), free choice and the feeling of autonomy that will be gained.

- Build on extrinsic motivation: health, money, respect (children and other family and friends (eg at pigeon events)

- Stress ability to achieve goals (pigeons), that he has no other bad habits, that he has progressed in DIY, that he always meets his targets at work, that his daughter can do it so he can too.

- Discuss family values and his role as provider and nurturer.

- ☐ Use future pacing to see himself getting over the obstacle of his friends at the pub potentially putting pressure on. Reinforce happiness and pride at being in control.

- ☐ Stress all pros and minimise cons (explain irritability and withdrawal and how they can be minimal with hypnosis and explain reasons why weight gain will not be a factor for him)

- ☐ Everything about becoming a non-smoker is positive and will feel good.

- ☐ Reinforce idea that he can have the identity of non-smoker (building on non-smoking times, eg night and at work)

- ☐ Raise awareness of habit element (but negate for him at the same time) and decrease belief in nicotine addiction (gently!)

- ☐ Using the Shavelson info, discuss areas where he is confident and how those where he isn't are ones where smoking is bringing him down. Map positive to the negative and future pace

- ☐ Stress positives from Harter: sociability, children, nurturing and providing

Weight Control

GOAL: weight

A client presenting for weight control, may have a well-defined goal (eg to lose 20lbs) or not. This process can help to clarify the goal if necessary and to firm up their reasons for deciding on this goal.

- ☐ direction - weight clients are likely to be wanting to move towards better health and fitness, perceived attractiveness, and greater self-acceptance. They are likely to be moving away from rejection, varying degrees of self-hate and illness. However, this is a distinctly variable area, so the particular needs of each client must be ascertained and not presumed.
- ☐ value - how important is meeting the goal? Does it fit with the client's value system?
- ☐ difficulty - how hard does the client feel it will be to achieve?
- ☐ identity - is the client's identity integral to either being the weight they are, or the weight they will be, or any behaviours that have led to the current situation? For example one client may have "always been big", while another may have "always been slim, until now". Behaviours are many and varied, but may be such things as being seen as "a drinker", or as the boss who always takes visitors out for big lunches.
- ☐ barriers - what obstacles are perceived by the client, and do you see any others that they have missed?
- ☐ orientation - if the client wants to lose weight for health, motivation may be task orientated, but it is more likely to be ego orientated. This shows the importance of ego-strengthening for weight clients
- ☐ support - does the client have support in making this change? For most weight clients, this is critical. Eating is, for most, a social activity, and the influence of family, friends and colleagues

can be profound. Of course, there are eating behaviours that are done alone, in which case the support required may be different.

- SMART - is the goal
  Specific? If the client simply wants to "feel better", help them to clarify what this means, at least more specifically
  Measurable? as with specific
  Adjustable? the adjustable element here is a need to recognise that a "bad day" does not mean the whole process is wrecked. The overall goal can remain the same, but the time factor may adjust due to circumstances
  Realistic? Crucial! If the client has a lot of weight to lose, set interim targets.
  There are also the clients whose expectations are unrealistic: for example the 50 year old who has always weighed 7 stone, but who now weighs 7 and a half and wants to lose the 7lbs
  Time-based? a time-line needs to be created

CONTROL: weight

- where is the client's typical Locus of Control?
- specifically for this goal, where is their Locus of Control?
- how much control do they perceive they have over their eating and activity patterns and the outcome of those behaviours?
- how realistic do you feel their perceptions to be?

INTRINSIC MOTIVATION: weight

How much of the following would the process of reaching the goal bring the client?

- ☐ feeling of making a free choice- perhaps for weight, the feeling of being in control is a better one to encourage.
- ☐ interest- help the client to find healthy eating and activity interesting
- ☐ challenge- an easy one to promote!
- ☐ enjoyment- harder, but the more you can help the client to realise that healthy behaviours can be enjoyable, the better

How much would the process of reaching the goal, and the end result help meet the following needs?

- ☐ relatedness
- ☐ competence
- ☐ autonomy

EXTRINSIC MOTIVATION: weight

How much does the client agree with these statements?

- ☐ I must do it
- ☐ I should do it
- ☐ I want to do it
- ☐ It is important to me to do it

Unless the client has been told by a doctor that they must lose weight, they are very often in the latter category. This can be utilised.

GENERAL MOTIVATION: weight

How high does the client rate their own motivation?

- ☐ Globally
- ☐ Contextually
- ☐ Situationally

Give guidance by providing examples

ATTRIBUTIONS: weight

- ☐ does the client generally attribute success to internal or external factors?
- ☐ does the client generally attribute failure to internal or external factors?
- ☐ if the client has previously failed to lose weight, do they attribute this to internal or external factors?
- ☐ are there any signs of learned helplessness, generally or specifically to do with weight?

SELF-PERCEPTION: weight

- confidence - how confident is the client generally? How confident are they in their abilities with regard to healthy eating and being active?
- ability - do they tend towards an entity or incremental view? Do they believe they are capable of reaching the goal?
- outcome - do they believe that the planned behaviours will result in reaching the goal?
- success - do they have prior successes in similar areas (eg, giving up smoking, or losing weight before) that they can draw from?
- imitation - how can they learn from others who have successfully lost weight, and kept it off. You can use surface structure metaphors here.
- worthiness - do they feel they deserve to be slim?
- persuasion - is there anyone persuading them to reach the goal? If so, do they perceive this as helpful or not?
- Shavelson - chunk down the Social, Emotional and Physical domains of self-perception to find areas where the client feels particularly confident, or the opposite. This will give you the information you need to be specific in terms of encouraging their self-confidence
- Harter - look at the client's perception of competence or adequacy on the following: Sociability, Job competence, Appearance, Athletic ability, Intimate relationships. This gives you more information on which to build.

ATTITUDE: weight

- beliefs - how does losing weight fit the client's belief system?
- emotions - what emotions are linked to both success and failure in reaching the goal?
- behaviour - how does the client's current behaviour assist or hinder the process of reaching the goal?
- others - do others have an influence on the process of reaching the goal?
- habit - if unhealthy eating and activity habits are to be broken, how strong does the client perceive them to be? A tendency towards being habitual can be utilised in establishing good habits

PHYSIOLOGY: weight

- what physical feelings are associated with both the client's current position and the intended position on reaching the goal?

- does the client have sufficient knowledge of the physiological processes involved?

ENVIRONMENT: weight

- in what ways may the client's physical and social environment affect the process of moving towards their goal?
- when the goal is reached, will there be any conflict with their physical or social environment?

PROs and CONs: weight

Assist the client to draw up a list of all the pros and cons of achieving the goal. For each, ascertain:

- the perceived severity (how good or bad it will be)
- the perceived probability of this happening
- how much effect losing weight is likely to have to increase/reduce (as appropriate), the severity and/or likelihood of the outcome

Examine:
- approval and gains for the client
- approval and gains for others
- disapproval and losses for self
- disapproval and losses for others

Case example: weight control

Kathleen presented wishing to lose weight. She weighs 210 pounds, is 5 foot 4 inches tall, 40 years old, married with children aged 10 and 6. She works as a designer for a leading cosmetic company and this role involves considerable travel. She reports that she had gradually put on weight since becoming pregnant with her first child. Before that she had consistently weighed 130 pounds. She attributes her weight gain to having children, having an inconsistent pattern of living, having to eat on the run, and regular business meals. She also reports having no time to exercise.

GOAL:

Kathleen's goal is stated as to lose a total of 70 pounds over a period of a year. This works out at 1.35 pounds per week. Kathleen is aware that interim goals could be useful to help maintain motivation.

Direction: Kathleen wants to feel healthier, feel more attractive (both towards motivators) and to move away from a feeling that her children are ashamed of her and that her weight is interfering with her chances of promotion at work. She has been prompted to act by two situations, firstly seeing a photo of herself which had shocked her, and secondly, feeling squashed in an airplane seat when sitting next to another overweight passenger.

Value: Kathleen places a high value on reaching her goal. She stated that she "just hadn't realised how bad things had got". The goal fits well in her value system of taking care of oneself and being someone that she and others could be proud of. She feels that this is damaged at present.

Difficulty: She feels it will be difficult, but still achievable.

Identity: Kathleen's identity remains with the weight that she had been before her children. Her new weight did not fit her idea of herself as fit, attractive, capable and in control.

Barriers:
- Business meals
- How to eat while travelling
- The children's leftovers
- Eating for the sake of it when tired

Orientation: mostly ego. A small amount of task orientation as Kathleen expressed the expectation that eating well would be enjoyable and give a good feeling of being in control.

Support: Kathleen felt that she would have support but that it was not very significant. She felt that she simply had to get on and do this herself as she was always able to chose her own meals.

The goal is specific, measurable, adjustable, realistic and time oriented. Kathleen was aware that interim goals are important to increase the SMART value, and that the adjustable criterion was significant. She knew that there would be days where she could not stick completely to her targets, but these would be balanced by days where she could do more exercise, for example.

CONTROL:

Locus of control: highly internal for almost everything in her life.

Specifically: in the past she had externalised control for eating and exercise but was becoming aware that this was not the way to be.

I feel that her awareness of what is needed is realistic although wonder whether she will be able to adapt all the significant areas all at once. I have noted this as something to work with specifically.

INTRINSIC MOTIVATION:

Kathleen likes the idea of feeling in control of her eating as she recognises the link to the feeling of being in control of a design project. She expects the process of eating healthily to be interesting although she feels she will be missing out in the business meal environment. She is looking forward to the challenge, and feels that she will feel more connected to her family when the goal is achieved, although not necessarily while the process is underway.

She understands that to take on this challenge could help her feeling of competence and autonomy. She has not felt these in relation to her eating before, but has simply ignored that this did not fit with her usual way of being.

EXTRINSIC MOTIVATION:

When I asked Kathleen this question, she answered with "I must do it": the external regulation answer. However, this did not fit with her previous answers so I questioned some more and it turned out that she felt so strongly integrated that the phrase "It is important to me" had not felt strong enough. Her "must" is from within.

GENERAL MOTIVATION:

Global: high

Contextual: high

Situational: high

ATTRIBUTIONS:

Generally, Kathleen attributes success and failure internally. She recognises that sometimes she takes this too far and takes responsibility for work problems which technically could be put down to other circumstances. Until this point however, she had attributed her weight gain to external sources, but recognises that this has been erroneous.

SELF-PERCEPTION:

Confidence: Kathleen is generally very confident. She knows that she is good at her job and believes herself to be a good wife and mother. She states that the only thing knocking her confidence is her realisation about her weight.

Ability: highly incremental. She believes that she has the ability and will achieve her goal

Outcome: Kathleen's planned behaviours are to control her food intake generally, to take healthy snacks with her when travelling, to choose healthy options from menus, to throw the children's leftovers away, and get a pedometer with the target of 10,000 steps per day. Kathleen believes that these behaviours will result in her goal being met.

Success: she has no similar successes to draw upon, although she has always been able to control her alcohol intake. However, she generally succeeds in projects she undertakes.

Imitation: Kathleen could not think of anyone that she knew who had lost much weight.

Worthiness: She feels completely worthy of every aspect of the goal.

Persuasion: No one has directly influenced Kathleen's decision to pursue this goal although she feels sure that "everyone" will approve.

Shavelson: Kathleen is generally confident in all of the Social and Emotional domains. In the Physical domain she feels confident in the following areas:

- Hair
- General attractiveness (describes herself as "not exactly beautiful but good enough")
- Sexuality
- Dancing

She lacks confidence in her body, due to the weight, and in sporting activities. She early on stated that "no way was she going to swim or go to the gym".

Harter:

- Sociability: very competent
- Job competence: very competent
- Appearance: adequate (except for weight)
- Athletic ability: poor (but inconsequential)
- Intimate relationships: very competent

ATTITUDE:

Beliefs: losing weight absolutely fits her belief system

Emotions: many positive emotions were expressed as linked to the idea of success. The idea of failing to meet the goal is linked with disappointment, anger, desperation which were covered up with strong determination to ensure this did not happen.

Behaviour: current behaviours clearly hamper the process. Kathleen has thought through what needs to be changed. We found various behaviours that will assist:

- Avoidance of alcohol
- Liking of healthy foods
- Being the primary shopper for the family
- Having a dog to take on walks (currently the dog goes out with a neighbour at least once a day)

Others: at business meals she may be pressured to eat more or unhealthy options.

Habit: Kathleen does not believe her habits to be strongly ingrained; just behaviours she had "fallen into".

PHYSIOLOGY:

Physical feelings: at the point when Kathleen decided to take action she had began to feel the physical effects of being overweight, finding activity difficult and recognising that many everyday behaviours (including putting on tights and having a bath) were harder than they should have been. She is looking forward to feeling fitter and more agile.

Knowledge: Kathleen is very knowledgeable about nutrition and the benefits of exercise.

ENVIRONMENT:

Kathleen's physical environment will present both challenges and opportunities. She has determined to utilise particularly the opportunities to be active presented while at work (in a large complex) and travelling. For example she would walk around while waiting in airports rather than sit in a café!

Kathleen does not feel that her social environment will be a particular issue during the process or after her goal has been reached as she feels equipped to deal with any pressure to over indulge.

PROS:

- Feel more attractive: very good and very likely
- Be more "acceptable" (Kathleen's words) to her children: very good and very likely
- Feel fitter: very good and very likely
- Get promotion: very good and possible
- Pride at taking control: very good and very likely

CONS:

- Feel deprived in business meals: bad and likely
- Be more stressed due to having to find time to exercise: bad and likely
- Inconvenience of having to plan when travelling: bad and very likely

Kathleen will gain (she believes) approval from her husband, her children and her bosses (who would be influenced by their perception that she will be more acceptable to her clients) She will also gain health and generally feel better about herself. She believes that her family will also benefit and, interestingly, that her children will gain approval from their friends from having a slim mother.

The only losses perceived are as listed in the cons. There is no perceived disapproval, except perhaps that business contacts may feel uncomfortable if she ate healthily when they were not.

Intervention:

This information was used to create the following suggestions (please note we are not giving the specific wording so as not to unduly influence you. Each hypnotist needs to complete this process in their own style):

- Guided imagery of Kathleen during the process of losing weight, being in control, enjoying her meals, enjoying walking with dog and without (including in foreign cities she visits, mentioning keeping safe), wandering around airports, being surprised and pleased at the total on her pedometer, eating sensibly at business meals, deflecting pressure to overeat.

- Guided imagery of when goal has been met. Visualise children and husband's reactions, see differences at work and in how she feels physically and emotionally, see specifics of getting in the bath, putting on her tights and flying next to an overweight passenger. See a photo taken a year hence and feel the pride.

- Reframe the perceived deprivation at business meals with metaphor to show that false friends should be rejected.

- Stress pleasure in choosing healthy food, planning for travelling, how eating when tired doesn't help, what to do with children's waste.

- Reinforce the integrated regulation.

- Discuss perception of competence, autonomy and relatedness that will be achieved, how she can enjoy the process as well as the end result. Build on perception of a challenge that can be met.

- Indirectly mention rewards of success (as stated in her goal), also possibly clothes (guided imagery of wearing what she would like to wear)

- Map over general success process to this goal

- Stress value of the goal to fit with value and belief system

- Discuss stimuli (tiredness, availability, pressure, hunger while travelling) and how alternative strategies decided will be beneficial, appropriate and result in feeling of control and pleasure

- Emphasise pros, negate cons (deprivation, time to exercise (will give her more energy so will be able to use other time more effectively and will relieve stress, also endorphins) and inconvenience)

- Reaffirm identity as attractive, in control, successful person

- ☐ Discuss needs for support, maybe asking for it if it becomes necessary.

- ☐ Build on positive aspects of the environment, dog, office buildings, airports, cities

- ☐ Emphasise Kathleen's ability to take control, attribute to internal processes, make choices

- ☐ Shavelson: stress positives, map over to perception of her body as it's becoming

- ☐ Harter: map over competencies

- ☐ Use surface structure metaphor(s) as she has no one to model

- ☐ Map over ability to control alcohol onto food

Performance enhancement: Sport

GOAL: sport

Goals for sport will vary widely. One client may have the goal of winning the Olympic gold medal, while another has the goal of completing a fun run.

- ◻ direction - here we need to look at why the client wishes to achieve their set goal. Usually, for sport this will be a "towards" goal, but remember there can be "away from" elements too, for example the sportsman who is wanting to avoid failure
- ◻ value - how important is meeting the goal? Does it fit with the client's value system?
- ◻ difficulty - how hard does the client feel it will be to achieve? Is this realistic? For example, many teenagers will set the goal of playing for their country, when few will succeed. Maybe they can, but intermediate goals may be helpful
- ◻ identity - is the client's identity integral to the sport in question? How can you utilise this?
- ◻ barriers - what obstacles are perceived by the client, and do you see any others that they have missed?
- ◻ orientation - is this goal primarily ego or task orientated?
- ◻ support - does the client have support in striving for this goal?
- ◻ SMART - is the goal
  Specific ?
  Measurable ?
  Adjustable?
  Realistic?
  Time-based?
  It is your role to help the client ensure that their sporting goal, meets these criteria. However, it is a good thing to have long term goals (or dreams) that do not fit the SMART acronym, but use SMART goals to take steps towards the dream.

CONTROL: sport

- ☐ where is the client's typical Locus of Control?
- ☐ specifically for this goal, where is their Locus of Control?
- ☐ how much control do they perceive they have over their behaviour and the outcome of that behaviour? For example, a golfer may perceive that she has control of her play, but not of the outcome as she cannot influence the play of her competitor. Whatever the perceptions, the client can be assisted to maximise their control
- ☐ how realistic do you feel their perceptions to be?

INTRINSIC MOTIVATION: sport

How much of the following would the process of reaching the goal bring the client?

- ☐ feeling of making a free choice
- ☐ interest
- ☐ challenge
- ☐ enjoyment

How much would the process of reaching the goal, and the end result help meet the following needs?

- ☐ relatedness
- ☐ competence
- ☐ autonomy

EXTRINSIC MOTIVATION: sport

How much does the client agree with these statements?

- ☐ I must do it
- ☐ I should do it
- ☐ I want to do it
- ☐ It is important to me to do it

Few sporting goals would be considered as "musts" or "shoulds", although be aware that sometimes the importance to the individual is so strong that this is interpreted in this way. For example, a leading English rugby player was recently quoted as saying "we must beat Australia: we have no choice".

GENERAL MOTIVATION: sport

How high does the client rate their own motivation?

- ☐ Globally
- ☐ Contextually
- ☐ Situationally

Give guidance by providing examples

ATTRIBUTIONS: sport

- ☐ does the client generally attribute success to internal or external factors?
- ☐ does the client generally attribute failure to internal or external factors?
- ☐ if the client has previously failed to reach this goal, do they attribute this to internal or external factors?
- ☐ are there any signs of learned helplessness, generally or specifically to this goal?

SELF-PERCEPTION: sport

- confidence - how confident is the client generally? How confident are they in their sporting abilities necessary to reach the goal?
- ability - do they tend towards an entity or incremental view? Do they believe they are capable of reaching the goal?
- outcome - do they believe that the planned behaviour will result in reaching the goal? Please note, that in order to reach any sporting goal, behaviours will have to be appropriate. Sometimes clients forget this!
- success - do they have prior successes in similar areas they can draw from?
- imitation - the client will know of others who have achieved this goal, even if not necessarily in exactly the same way. Encourage them to learn from their experience
- worthiness - do they feel they deserve to reach the goal?
- persuasion - is there anyone persuading them to reach the goal? If so, do they perceive this as helpful or not?
- Shavelson - chunk down the Social, Emotional and Physical domains of self-perception to find areas where the client feels particularly confident, or the opposite. This will give you the information you need to be specific in terms of encouraging their self-confidence
- Harter - look at the client's perception of competence or adequacy on the following: Sociability, Appearance, and Athletic ability,as appropriate. This gives you more information on which to build.

ATTITUDE: sport

- ☐ beliefs - how does meeting the goal fit the client's belief system?
- ☐ emotions - what emotions are linked to both success and failure in reaching the goal?
- ☐ behaviour - how do the client's current behaviours assist or hinder the process of reaching the goal?
- ☐ others - do others have an influence on the process of reaching the goal?
- ☐ habit - habits may be a factor in aiding or hindering the process of reaching the goal. How can this element be maximised to assist the client?

ENVIRONMENT: sport

- ☐ in what ways may the client's physical and social environment affect the process of moving towards their goal?
- ☐ when the goal is reached, will there be any conflict with their physical or social environment?

PHYSIOLOGY: sport

- ☐ what physical feelings are associated with both the client's current position and the intended position on reaching the goal?

- ☐ does the client have sufficient knowledge of the physiological processes involved?

PROs and CONs: sport

Assist the client to draw up a list of all the pros and cons of achieving the goal. For each, ascertain:

- the perceived severity (how good or bad it will be)
- the perceived probability of this happening
- how much effect the behaviour is likely to have to increase/reduce (as appropriate), the severity and/or likelihood of the outcome

Examine:

- approval and gains for the client
- approval and gains for others
- disapproval and losses for self
- disapproval and losses for others

Note that particularly for lofty sporting goals, the client may have not consciously recognised the negative consequences of success; the clearer they can become the less this will unconsciously interfere

Case example: sport

Rex is a 27 year old engineer who plays golf in his spare time. He has a handicap of 11, but regularly plays much better than this if playing alone. He enters competitions at his local club, but gets frustrated at his performance. He reports that he has never had to try very hard to achieve anything he has attempted, and often can't be bothered to practise his golf. His fiancée is not keen on his hobby as it takes him away from her too much.

GOAL:

Rex states his goal to be reducing his handicap to 5 within the next twelve months. In order to do this he knows he must find the motivation to practise and find out what is blocking him from playing well in company.

Direction: the goal is towards success and achievement and away from frustration. Rex is also keen to avoid what he perceives as failure in that he is used to being the best in whatever he has done (school, university, his career)

Value: Rex values golf highly, and success very highly.

Difficulty: he believes it will be easy, "with a bit of help", because everything is easy "if you put your mind to it". I am not sure that his perspective is realistic enough, and discuss broadening the goal to include amount of practice and other measures than total shots per round (eg average number of puts, analysis of different strokes, clubs, errors).

Identity: Rex considers himself "a golfer". He identifies with every aspect of the sport including the social side of the club.

Barriers:

- Rex's fiancée is an obvious barrier to achievement, but Rex was initially dismissive of this. In discussion he realised he needed to find a way to resolve the issue and he decided to encourage her to accompany him as much as possible and maybe even to take up the sport herself
- Laziness
- Attitude of expecting success to arrive with no effort

Orientation: strongly ego: the result is "all that matters". Rex expressed the opinion that he would rather play badly and win than play well and lose.

Support: no support unless he does well enough to be in his club's team.

The goal is specific, measurable, adjustable (although this needs some work in Rex's model of the world), fairly realistic and time oriented.

CONTROL:

Locus of control: typically Rex feels in control of his destiny. He feels that his successes have been due to inherent ability and skill.

Specifically: he struggles to balance his belief that he has skill as a golfer with the fact that he has not done well enough. If he was to suggest that the outcome of his goal related to luck he feels he would be abdicating responsibility, but he doesn't like the idea that he may not be able to do it.

He is clear, however, that no one else can control his ability as a golfer, and also, significantly, that however well he plays he cannot control the outcome of any particular match as he cannot control the other players' play.

INTRINSIC MOTIVATION:

Rex has little intrinsic motivation to play golf itself, but he has in the whole process, eg belonging to the club, the camaraderie, the status. He refers to the actual play as "usually frustrating" and "rarely enjoyable". The challenge aspect frightens him somewhat.

EXTRINSIC MOTIVATION:

He agreed with the identified regulation level: "I want to". He felt that this was more empowering than saying it was important to him. I felt he was wobbling a little with a worry of "what if..."

GENERAL MOTIVATION:

Global: high

Contextual: high

Situational: high

ATTRIBUTIONS:

Generally, Rex attributes success internally and failure externally. His only non-golf example of failure was failing his driving test the first time, but this was due to "an examiner who judged him for having a sporty car". When asked to what he attributes previous negative experiences in golf, all I got was "I don't know, I can't explain it".

SELF-PERCEPTION:

Confidence: generally Rex is highly confident, and he believes he has the inherent ability, although this waivers as he cannot reconcile this with the fact that he is not succeeding.

Ability: he has an entity view of ability. He feels he has always achieved because he was born with high ability in the areas he has addressed. He commented that he was hopeless at cross-words and nothing could change that.

Outcome: Rex is aware that he is going to have to adopt new behaviours if he is to meet his goal, ie practise consistently. He had expected that he could just become successful without this but he has learnt that this is necessary. He believes that if he does this he MUST then succeed.

Success: many prior successes he can draw from, but not with the required effort.

Imitation: I asked who he particularly admired in the golfing world. He said Tiger Woods because of his natural ability. He did not seem aware that Tiger has worked exceptionally hard since being a small child to develop this natural ability! I asked what he thought of Vijay Singh and while he admires him he does not value his success as much as he has had to work so hard to achieve it.

Worthiness: not surprisingly Rex feels worthy of achieving his goal, although there is that worry: "what if I am not up to it?"

Persuasion: no one is persuading Rex towards this goal.

Shavelson: in the social domain Rex is always confident, in the emotional he is confident except that he knows there must be an emotional element to his failure to perform with others when he is ok alone. This question raised an interesting piece of information; that is that he used not to participate in karaoke, but that he had been persuaded by his fiancée and now loves it.

In the physical domain, Rex felt confident in terms of:

- Strength
- Attractiveness
- Fitness

But lacked confidence in anything that "requires grace, like dancing".

Harter:
- Sociability: very competent
- Appearance: more than adequate
- Athletic ability: very competent

ATTITUDE:

Beliefs: this goal fits very much into his belief system. Success is paramount. However this is "supposed to be achieved without effort".

Emotions: if he achieves his goal, Rex expects to feel good, confident, fulfiled, and get a good feeling of being part of the club. If he were not to achieve the goal he described the expected feeling as "unbearable: I would have to stop playing and do something else."

Behaviour: Rex's minimal practice definitely hinders reaching the goal. The following behaviours help:

- The practice that he does do
- Eating well and drinking little alcohol
- Going to the gym
- Reading about golf and watching it on TV

Others: his fiancée has an influence which could be negative unless appropriately addressed. There are no others at present with an influence although this question prompted Rex to consider whether to take more lessons (although that feels currently like admitting defeat), or finding a playing partner who can support him on a regular basis.

Habit: many of Rex's working behaviours are habitual, so he is wondering whether his practice can become so.

PHYSIOLOGY:

Physical feelings: the only difference in physical feelings identified was that he felt that he wouldn't experience the adrenaline that he currently does during competitions if he met his goal.

ENVIRONMENT:

The problem in terms of environment is again with his fiancée, but this is being addressed. Otherwise the impact of social and physical environments will not change.

PROS:

- Good feelings: success, achievement, pride: very good and very likely
- Enjoy the game itself more: very good and likely
- Be pleased to have met the challenge: good and likely
- Better relationships in the club: good and likely
- Possibility of more golfing opportunities: good and possible

CONS:

- May annoy fiancée: bad and possible

There could be many gains and much approval for Rex, but there could also be disapproval from his fiancée. She may also lose out.

Intervention:

This information was used to create the following suggestions (please note we are not giving the specific wording so as not to unduly influence you. Each hypnotist needs to complete this process in their own style):

- Guided imagery to encourage Rex to see himself enjoying his golf with others as well as when alone, to see the game itself as a good experience, visualise handing in cards, with the accompanying good feelings of success and pride. Ask him to see himself meeting the challenge of setting up the practising habits and how that will feel good as he is taking control, it is empowering, show him his relationships both at the club and at home improving, see himself relaxed as he plays in competitions and future pace to the opening up of opportunities.

- Look at set backs as experience to learn from. Bad shots and even bad rounds are necessary to develop. You may be able to learn bunker shots in practice, but they are different in the pressure of a match, so they give you an opportunity to learn.

- Emphasise different measures of progress, putting, different shots and clubs, errors etc (not too specific, he needs to choose)

- Reframe his belief that this could be difficult to the opportunity to meet a challenge. Site models from other walks of life who are admired for striving (again be vague with indirect language)

- Map habituality from work onto golf practice: increase perceived value of practice and enjoyment of that.

- Highlight intrinsic elements of competence, relatedness and autonomy (what can be more autonomous that playing golf?)

- Look at the perceived negative effect of playing with others. Compare to karaoke and utilise techniques to enable him to feel alone if he needs to even when people are around.

- Work on identity as a golfer, but separate from specific competence and move to general (all golfers have bad days, site examples of pros. Visualise possibility of one day becoming a scratch golfer OR club captain (give choice and only possibility)

- Emphasise how his relationship with his fiancée can improve and how she will be likely to be happier with him if he is more relaxed and less frustrated as he succeeds.

- Seek positive influences including the pros he watches on TV and perhaps leading members of the club.

- Reframe laziness as being against his values. Relaxing and being chilled is different! They fit.

- Address the issue of his belief that he is not graceful. Tie to specific of dancing, separate from golf. This is a different sort of grace (perhaps he needs to know that it can still be macho?)

- Reinforce his good behaviours and their positive influence (going to the gym, eating well, drinking little, observing golf)

Performance enhancement: Learning

GOAL: learning

Learning goals are often inherently extrinsic in that they are about the end result, or the consequences of this. For example it is common for the goal to be to study for a degree in order to get a particular job. Many people are, of course, intrinsically motivated to learn, but they are less likely to seek you out.

- ☐ direction - movement is usually towards the result, but can also include a process of moving away from such things as failure, poverty and feelings of inadequacy
- ☐ value - how important is meeting the goal? Does it fit with the client's value system? A particular area of interest here is for those who do not value learning, but value the end result (eg a better paid job or higher status)
- ☐ difficulty - how hard does the client feel it will be to achieve?
- ☐ identity - is the client's identity linked to either being a learner, or an achiever or not? If a client has gone through the school system labelled negatively, switching to being the one who studies may be quite a shift. Remember also that identities associated with success and hard work can often be perceived negatively: for example, use of the word "swat"
- ☐ barriers - what obstacles are perceived by the client, and do you see any others that they have missed?
- ☐ orientation - is this goal primarily ego or task orientated?
- ☐ support - does the client have support in making this change?
- ☐ SMART - is the goal
  Specific ?
  Measurable ?
  Adjustable?
  Realistic?
  Time-based?

CONTROL: learning

- ☐ where is the client's typical Locus of Control?
- ☐ specifically for this goal, where is their Locus of Control?
- ☐ how much control do they perceive they have over their learning and the outcome of that behaviour?
- ☐ how realistic do you feel their perceptions to be?

INTRINSIC MOTIVATION: learning

How much of the following would the process of reaching the goal bring the client?

- ☐ feeling of making a free choice
- ☐ interest
- ☐ challenge
- ☐ enjoyment

How much would the process of reaching the goal, and the end result help meet the following needs?

- ☐ relatedness
- ☐ competence
- ☐ autonomy

EXTRINSIC MOTIVATION: learning

How much does the client agree with these statements?

- ☐ I must do it
- ☐ I should do it
- ☐ I want to do it
- ☐ It is important to me to do it

Clients presenting with this issue are likely to be more on the "must" or "should" end of the continuum. It is important however, not to presume. You have the opportunity to help the client move towards the other end.

GENERAL MOTIVATION: learning

How high does the client rate their own motivation?

- ☐ Globally
- ☐ Contextually
- ☐ Situationally

Give guidance by providing examples

ATTRIBUTIONS: learning

- ☐ does the client generally attribute success to internal or external factors?
- ☐ does the client generally attribute failure to internal or external factors?
- ☐ if the client has previously failed to reach this goal, do they attribute this to internal or external factors?
- ☐ are there any signs of learned helplessness, generally or specifically to learning?

SELF-PERCEPTION: learning

- ☐ confidence - how confident is the client generally? How confident are they in the behaviours necessary to reach the goal?
- ☐ ability - do they tend towards an entity or incremental view? Do they believe they are capable of reaching the goal?
- ☐ outcome - do they believe that studying will result in reaching the goal?
- ☐ success - do they have prior successes in similar areas they can draw from?
- ☐ imitation - they are likely to have people to model, but if not, you can be a model for them.
- ☐ worthiness - do they feel they deserve to reach the goal?
- ☐ persuasion - is there anyone persuading them to reach the goal? If so, do they perceive this as helpful or not?
- ☐ Shavelson - chunk down the Academic domain of self-perception, and any others that are relevant to find areas where the client feels particularly confident, or the opposite. This will give you the information you need to be specific in terms of encouraging their self-confidence
- ☐ Harter - look at the client's perception of competence/adequacy on the Harter domains,as appropriate. This gives you more information on which to build.

ATTITUDE: learning

- beliefs - how does meeting the goal fit the client's belief system?
- emotions - what emotions are linked to both success and failure in reaching the goal?
- behaviour - how does the client's current behaviour assist or hinder the process of reaching the goal?
- others - do others have an influence on the process of reaching the goal?
- habit - a particular habit that may be relevant here is procrastination. This often is a huge influence on the process of learning

PHYSIOLOGY: learning

- what physical feelings, if any, are associated with both the client's current position and the intended position on reaching the goal?

- are there any physiological processes involved? If so, does the client understand them?

ENVIRONMENT: learning

- in what ways may the client's physical and social environment affect the process of moving towards their goal?
- when the goal is reached, will there be any conflict with their physical or social environment?

PROs and CONs: learning

Assist the client to draw up a list of all the pros and cons of achieving the goal. For each, ascertain:

- the perceived severity (how good or bad it will be)
- the perceived probability of this happening
- how much effect studying or reaching the goal is likely to have to increase/reduce (as appropriate), the severity and/or likelihood of the outcome

Examine:
- approval and gains for the client
- approval and gains for others
- disapproval and losses for self
- disapproval and losses for others

Case example: learning

Pamela is a 31 year old marketing manager for a publishing company. The company has just taken over a French publishing house. She has been told that if she wants to keep her job (which she loves), she will have to spend a week or so every month liaising with her French colleagues. While Pamela was very successful academically, she "just couldn't do French".

GOAL:

Pamela's goal is to overcome her issues with learning French and so become a confident speaker of the language.

Direction: Pamela's goal is towards success and confidence and away from the "pain and discomfort" of not being able to speak French

Value: She puts a very high value on her job, but otherwise would not put a high value on speaking French. She stated "I've always got by when I've been there. I travel a lot and I can't learn every language in the world"

Difficulty: Pamela believes that meeting this goal will be very difficult indeed.

Identity: Her identity is very much tied in with her work. She is a single woman, no children and sees herself as a "career woman".

Barriers: the only barrier identified is Pamela's lack of belief in the possibility of success.

Orientation: at this stage Pamela just wants the outcome, she is not motivated ego-wise at all, or interested in the task itself.

Support: she has the support of her boss, but this feels more like pressure. Other people around her are uninterested.

The goal needs some work on it's SMART-ness. Pamela needs to think about what "competent" means, how it is to be measured, and when she needs to have met the goal. It is clearly not an adjustable goal (she can't change it to German instead!), and the realistic element is one that can be worked on in therapy.

CONTROL:

Locus of control: generally Pamela has an internal locus of control.

Specifically: for this goal there is no feeling of control. She believes it to be almost unachievable. However she can control how she learns in that she has been given carte blanche for the arrangements and she has found a woman that she feels she can trust to work with one to one.

INTRINSIC MOTIVATION:

This is a problem area although this gives scope for building motivation. One aim would be to introduce the idea that working on this goal can bring about feelings of competence, interest, enjoyment and to build on the challenge element. Also, Pamela can be helped to envisage herself relating well to a whole new group of people in the French office and beyond.

EXTRINSIC MOTIVATION:

Pamela is at the External Regulation end of the extrinsic continuum. A task of therapy is to move her towards the other end.

GENERAL MOTIVATION:

Global: high

Contextual: high for work and learning in general

Situational: low for learning French

ATTRIBUTIONS:

Generally, Pamela attributes both success and failure to internal factors. Specifically with regard to languages, she attributes her failure to learn to the fact that she "just doesn't have the ability", a highly internal factor. It is clear that this is a case of learned helplessness as she describes her experiences of school which lead her to develop this belief.

SELF-PERCEPTION:

Confidence: Pamela is generally quietly confident, and is a competent learner: she has many qualifications at a high level, but she has no confidence on this specifically.

Ability: for this Pamela holds an entity view, but has an incremental view on other forms of learning.

Outcome: she does not currently believe that undertaking lessons will result in her goal being met.

Success: she has many prior learning successes, and significantly, she learnt to speak English as a small child! She has, of course, not recognised that this is the same thing.

Imitation: Pamela has a close friend who has become fluent in Italian since marrying a mutual friend from Rome.

Worthiness: she feels worthy of the goal in that she is absolutely committed to her career.

Persuasion: Pamela's boss is being heavily persuasive, in a kindly way, but one that leaves no room for manoeuvre. It feels like pressure.

Shavelson:

- Academic domain: Pamela feels highly competent in many academic areas, and highly incompetent in foreign languages. However, she prides herself on her communication skills, both orally and in writing and on always being grammatically correct.

Harter:

- Job competence: highly competent
- Intelligence: highly competent

ATTITUDE:

Beliefs: the end result of achieving the goal will fit with Pamela's belief system in that she is career minded and achievement in this field is all important. She also believes it important to strive and to not give in, so this can be utilised for working on this goal.

Emotions: Success is currently linked to relief and failure to fear about finding another job, rejection, anger at herself and resignation

Behaviour: Currently, behaviours are not particularly relevant as Pamela does not do anything that helps or hinders the process.

Others: the teacher that Pamela has chosen will have a significant influence on the process, as does her boss who is pressurising her to achieve the goal.

Habit: Pamela's habit of always completing tasks within deadline could be helpful.

ENVIRONMENT:

Pamela's environment will have little impact on her progress towards her goal. However, this question prompted her to wonder if she could ask to visit the French office for a period of weeks a little way along the line to immerse herself in the language. This was the first point at which she even so much as hinted that she may achieve the goal.

PROS:

- Keep her job: wonderful and certain

The following are ones to suggest but that Pamela herself has not mentioned:

- Feeling of pleasure, pride, competence from achieving: good and very likely
- Feeling of enjoyment and interest: good and possible
- Relatedness that will come with working in France: good and likely

CONS:

There are no cons to achieving the goal, and just the perceived "agony" of having the lessons as the process.

The gains for Pamela are vicarious. Her main goal is to keep her job, not to gain anything additionally. However she will get the approval of her boss. There are no perceived losses or disapproval for herself or others.

Intervention:

This information was used to create the following suggestions (please note we are not giving the specific wording so as not to unduly influence you. Each hypnotist needs to complete this process in their own style):

- Guided imagery showing Pamela enjoying her lessons, practising and then speaking freely and comfortably with French colleagues and in other environments in France. Build in feelings of pride, pleasure, fun, achievement, and relatedness and stress how she will be avoiding the pain of failure.

- Discuss the fact that she learnt to speak English as a child, and how she made mistakes and that was ok, but she gradually got better by listening, trying things out, finding ways to express herself and reading until she has reached the high level of skill that she possesses now.

- Reframe past experience. Encourage her to share the responsibility for her learned helplessness with her teachers and any others who had an influence. Show her how different this experience was to when she learnt English, and how unrepresentative it is in her life.

- Build on her identity as being capable. Map over incremental view from other learning to this situation. Help her to realise that there are a million (or so!) steps she needs to take, but that each is simple. Strengthen her belief in her learning abilities based on previous challenges that she has achieved.

- Encourage the SMART factors that are being developed for the goal.

- Discuss her relationship with the teacher and future pace how this will grow and strengthen.

- Using emotional constructs, help Pamela towards the integrated regulation end of the extrinsic motivation continuum.

- Utilise her habit of working to deadlines to help her to realise that she can schedule her study time; mentally rehearse and include fun and safety.

- Help Pamela to take charge of her challenge and to "take it away from" her boss. That is, to decide for herself that this is something she is going to do, thus reducing the power of his pressure

Performance enhancement: Creativity

GOAL: creativity

In this section we include art, music, drama and any other process that is primarily creative and for which the client is working towards a goal.Typically this may be someone who is struggling with stage fright, writer's block or lack of confidence in their ability.

- ☐ direction - creative goals are usually "towards" goals: the client is usually seeking success or fulfilment in a creative area
- ☐ value - how important is meeting the goal? Does it fit with the client's value system?
- ☐ difficulty - how hard does the client feel it will be to achieve?
- ☐ identity - is the client's identity integral to the creative process or result as is, or as will be?
- ☐ barriers - what obstacles are perceived by the client, and do you see any others that they have missed?
- ☐ orientation - is this goal primarily ego or task orientated?
- ☐ support - does the client have support in making this change?
- ☐ SMART - is the goal
  Specific ?
  Measurable ?
  Adjustable?
  Realistic?
  Time-based?

CONTROL: creativity

- ☐ where is the client's typical Locus of Control?
- ☐ specifically for this creative process, where is their Locus of Control?
- ☐ how much control do they perceive they have over their creativity and the outcome of that creativity?
- ☐ how realistic do you feel their perceptions to be?

INTRINSIC MOTIVATION: creativity

How much of the following would the process of reaching the goal bring the client?

- ☐ feeling of making a free choice
- ☐ interest
- ☐ challenge
- ☐ enjoyment

How much would the process of reaching the goal, and the end result help meet the following needs?

- ☐ relatedness
- ☐ competence
- ☐ autonomy

EXTRINSIC MOTIVATION: creativity

How much does the client agree with these statements?

- ☐ I must do it
- ☐ I should do it
- ☐ I want to do it
- ☐ It is important to me to do it

Clients are more likely to be towards the "important" end of this continuum, but as with sports people, the process may be SO important to the client that it is perceived by them as a "must". You need to differentiate.

GENERAL MOTIVATION: creativity

How highly does the client rate their own motivation?

- ☐ Globally
- ☐ Contextually
- ☐ Situationally

Give guidance by providing examples

ATTRIBUTIONS: creativity

- ☐ does the client generally attribute success to internal or external factors?
- ☐ does the client generally attribute failure to internal or external factors?
- ☐ if the client has previously failed to reach this goal, do they attribute this to internal or external factors?
- ☐ are there any signs of learned helplessness, generally or specifically to this goal?

SELF-PERCEPTION: creativity

- confidence - how confident is the client generally? How confident are they in the behaviours necessary to reach the goal?
- ability - do they tend towards an entity or incremental view? Do they believe they are capable of reaching the goal?
- outcome - do they believe that the planned behaviour will result in reaching the goal?
- success - do they have prior successes in similar areas they can draw from?
- imitation - they will almost certainly know of others who have achieved this goal. A good opportunity for modelling
- worthiness - do they feel they deserve to reach the goal?
- persuasion - is there anyone persuading them to reach the goal? If so, do they perceive this as helpful or not?
- Shavelson - chunk down the appropriate domains of self-perception to find areas where the client feels particularly confident, or the opposite. None of the defined domains may be suitable, in which case define your own. This will give you the information you need to be specific in terms of encouraging their self-confidence
- Harter - look at the client's perception of competence or adequacy on the Harter domains,as appropriate. This gives you more information on which to build.

ATTITUDE: creativity

- ☐ beliefs - how does meeting the goal fit the client's belief system?
- ☐ emotions - what emotions are linked to both success and failure in reaching the goal?
- ☐ behaviour - how does the client's current behaviour assist or hinder the process of reaching the goal?
- ☐ others - do others have an influence on the process of reaching the goal?
- ☐ habit - procrastination may be a factor, as may unhelpful routines. Good habits can be instilled.

PHYSIOLOGY: creativity

- ☐ what physical feelings, if any, are associated with both the client's current position and the intended position on reaching the goal?

- ☐ are any physiological processes involved? If so, does the client understand them?

ENVIRONMENT: creativity

- ☐ in what ways may the client's physical and social environment affect the process of moving towards their goal?
- ☐ when the goal is reached, will there be any conflict with their physical or social environment?

PROs and CONs: creativity

Assist the client to draw up a list of all the pros and cons of achieving the goal. For each, ascertain:

- ☐ the perceived severity (how good or bad it will be)
- ☐ the perceived probability of this happening
- ☐ how much effect the process and goal is likely to have to increase/reduce (as appropriate), the severity and/or likelihood of the outcome

Examine:

- ☐ approval and gains for the client
- ☐ approval and gains for others
- ☐ disapproval and losses for self
- ☐ disapproval and losses for others

Case example: creativity

Harvey is a classically trained pianist who since leaving music college has taken a string of low paid jobs while attempting to get bookings as a concert pianist. He has had no luck on this at ali and is now thinking of changing tack and becoming a cocktail lounge pianist. His agent says that these jobs are easier to come by and can be relatively secure employment. However, Harvey will need to extend his repertoire and style base to include jazz and popular music. He finds the idea challenging but exciting. He is seeking help as he feels he will struggle with the change of style.

GOAL:

Harvey's goal is to take lessons in some new styles of music, to develop his own style of presentation and to get a job in a cocktail lounge or similar within a year.

Direction: Harvey's goal is very much a "towards" goal: toward success, stability, and fulfilment. There is, of course, an away element: away from dull, unfulfilling jobs and dissatisfaction.

Value: Harvey places a high value on meeting this goal.

Difficulty: he does not believe it will be very difficult to achieve, once he has overcome his concerns about the change, although he is aware that factors outside of his control may affect his chances of getting any particular job.

Identity: Harvey's identity has "always" been tied into being a musician, and specifically a pianist. He is happy with the idea of this identity mutating from the unfulfilled concert pianist to what he says he will term "professional pianist", but feels that his parents will be disappointed not to be able to refer to him in the old way when talking about him to their friends.

Barriers: Harvey could not identify any possible barriers to success except his own fear of change and doubt as to whether he can perform adequately in the different styles.

Orientation: this goal is highly task and ego-oriented.

Support: he has the support of his partner who is also looking for stability in life.

The goal is fairly specific, fairly measurable (although the style elements are hard to quantify), adjustable , realistic and time oriented.

CONTROL:

Locus of control: Harvey struggled with this concept, but came to realise that he feels in control of some areas of his life, but that at times he feels that his destiny is "in the lap of the gods".

Specifically: he feels that he can control the process of developing his style, and is looking forward to doing this (he has some unusual ideas for dress and presentation), but feels that fate has a role to play. Also he is strongly external in actually getting a job at the end of the process, which is probably a realistic place to be as he can only do his best and if he is not what a particular hotel or restaurant is looking for then his control over the outcome is limited.

INTRINSIC MOTIVATION:

There is significant intrinsic motivation in this goal. Harvey feels he will enjoy the process of developing and will find the resulting job fulfiling. He is interested in the various styles of music that he will be pursuing and feels nicely challenged by the process. He feels that achieving his goal will give him a feeling of competence and will help his feelings of relatedness as he likes the idea of the interaction that there will be with guests, rather than the typical concert situation where there is no such interaction.

EXTRINSIC MOTIVATION:

Harvey is in-between identified and integrated regulation. He wants to achieve this, and being a musician is important to him. He feels it would be a step too far to say that being this sort of musician is completely integrated, but he is hopeful that it will become so in time.

GENERAL MOTIVATION:

Global: low. Harvey does not generally see himself as highly motivated but describes himself as inherently "lazy and chilled".

Contextual: for music, high

Situational: for this goal, high

ATTRIBUTIONS:

Generally, Harvey attributes his successes to his own ability and effort, and failures to a mixture of lack of the same and luck or fate. Specifically in relation to his failure to make it as a concert pianist, he attributes this to him not being quite good enough, not classically good looking and to not being willing to "submerge his personality" enough.

SELF-PERCEPTION:

Confidence: Harvey is generally reasonably confident. He has high confidence as a musician, in fact he states that sometimes it is too high and he comes over as arrogant.

Ability: he has an incremental view of ability when it comes to music and believes that he can do this, although there is a hint of doubt.

Outcome: he feels fairly confident that by developing in the areas he has identified and getting over the fear attached to doing so, he will be able to get the job he wants. He has researched this by visiting top London hotels and restaurants and observing cocktail lounge pianists in action. He feels that he can do as well and provide something a little more in terms of the interaction that he intends to build in with the guests.

Success: he has previous successes in developing his creative skills to draw on, but nothing significant in terms of getting the job at the end; his successes in getting work have been either trivial auditions or trivial jobs.

Imitation: he has particular pianists in mind that he wishes to model, but he had not thought of the possibility of talking to any of them about what they do and how to get to this position. He liked this idea, but felt nervous about this in case they didn't want to talk to him or felt he was threatening him.

Worthiness: Harvey laughed at this question. He feels worthy of being the top concert pianist in the world, let alone to get this opportunity.

Persuasion: his partner is gently persuasive, but Harvey perceives this as useful and encouraging.

Shavelson: the domain that seems most relevant here is social in that the resulting job will require Harvey to relate to guests in a convivial manner and in chunking this down it seems that Harvey is very confident in this area, especially when "wearing his musician's hat". The academic domain can be adapted to look at his ability as a musician, but this was already not in dispute.

Harter:

- Sociability: competent
- Job competence: this is where Harvey will be working
- Physical appearance: adequate, needs to be "styled" to fit his new professional persona
- Sense of humour: competent. This was not something that he had mentioned, but this made him realise how important this could be, but he wanted to stress that although he wanted interaction he was not intending to be a cabaret act!

ATTITUDE:

Beliefs: there is a slight conflict with the belief system that had been in place which gave more value to classical music than other forms and to traditional styles of presentation than to the style that Harvey is now pursuing. He feels this will be an issue for his parents, but he himself is happy to move on. He finds it "freeing" and recognises that perhaps he was living to other people's belief systems rather than one he had thought out for himself.

Emotions: achieving the goal, and the process of working towards it will create feelings of pride, enjoyment, fulfilment, fun and challenge. Failure to reach the goal would create feelings of disappointment, regret and fear: "what now?"

Behaviour: Harvey's current practice schedule will be a very real benefit in his progress towards the goal. He reframed his laziness as giving himself space and time to concentrate on striving for this goal. His tendency towards behaving arrogantly could hinder the process, so some work on building real confidence rather than a mask will help.

Others: the music teachers that he chooses to involve will have an impact so they need to be chosen with care. Also, Harvey is aware that getting opinions from disinterested parties will be a useful influence and as he still has a lot of musical contacts from college he will build this into his plan.

Habit: Harvey's practice habit is a useful one, and is to be encouraged. He does not have any habits that would interfere.

ENVIRONMENT:

Harvey's physical environment is helpful in that he lives in a house where he can practise the piano at any time with little risk of disturbing anyone. He has a good quality piano located in a pleasant, comfortable room. His social environment fits well with the process of achieving the goal in that he can practise when his partner is at work and they can spend time together or with friends at other times.

When he has achieved his goal and is working, there may be conflict with timings, but he is willing to accept this, as is his partner who may then be able to work different hours to match Harvey's more closely than they would at present.

PROS:

- Stability: good and likely
- Fulfilment: good and likely
- Enjoyment: very good and likely
- Challenge: good and very likely

CONS:

- Not doing what he originally wanted to do: somewhat bad and likely
- Upsetting parents: somewhat bad and likely
- Difficult hours:somewhat bad and very likely
- Fear of failure: bad and possible

Intervention:

This information was used to create the following suggestions (please note we are not giving the specific wording so as not to unduly influence you. Each hypnotist needs to complete this process in their own style):

- Guided imagery to help Harvey see himself developing his new style, musically and presentation. Intensify the pleasurable emotions associated with the process, then move on to guiding him through some job selection processes. Perhaps he can see himself not getting one job, so that he can experience that this is ok, and then a successful one. Move on to let him experience the job utilising all his senses and emotions.

- Build in awareness of the hard work and risk involved in the changes, but frame these as positive, rewarding and exciting. Create a safety net for the risk; a safe place perhaps or a bubble to protect him from potential criticism.

- Strengthen his belief in his ability, mapping across from other musical successes. Stress the similarities, and how he has the right to make choices as to the value he puts on different musical styles and careers.

- Work on the identity of the professional pianist and how this fits his current life with his partner and how it will fit into their future together.

- Maximise the intrinsic motivation, both for the end goal and the process of achieving it.

- Compare this change to other changes that he has made to demonstrate that change is normal and natural but it is also normal and natural to feel some anxiety. He has changed before and it is ok, so he can do so again. Stress how we constantly change and GROW.

- Ask him to imagine the pianists he wishes to model and to consider what it is about them that makes them great. How can he integrate these behaviours and characteristics into himself?

- Utilise his imagery of "wearing his musician's hat", and his perception of his sense of humour to help him build confidence in the presentation of his work.

- Work with his feelings of control, particularly with regard to the help he will seek on the way, and in the way he approaches job applications. Get him to see himself behaving confidently, not arrogantly.

- Use guided visualisation to strengthen the practising habit, and perhaps (in consultation) to adapt this slightly to his new style, maybe wearing something different as he practises, or altering the layout of the room so that this can be anchored into the "new Harvey".

Personal development
Career planning

GOAL: careers

In this section we include not simply career planning itself but also financial planning. Some clients will have outcome goals of fulfilment in their career, others of financial reward. However, both can be maximised for most clients.

- ☐ direction - career goals are likely to have more of a "towards" orientation, but do not overlook the "away from" elements
- ☐ value - how important is meeting the goal? Does it fit with the client's value system?
- ☐ difficulty - how hard does the client feel it will be to achieve?
- ☐ identity - is the client's identity integral to the behaviours involved in reaching the goal, or the role associated with the career, as is, or as will be?
- ☐ barriers - what obstacles are perceived by the client, and do you see any others that they have missed?
- ☐ orientation - is this goal primarily ego or task orientated?
- ☐ support - does the client have support in striving for this goal?
- ☐ SMART - is the goal
  Specific ?
  Measurable ?
  Adjustable?
  Realistic?
  Time-based?

CONTROL: careers

- ☐ where is the client's typical Locus of Control?
- ☐ specifically for this goal, where is their Locus of Control?
- ☐ how much control do they perceive they have over their behaviour and the outcome of that behaviour?
- ☐ how realistic do you feel their perceptions to be?

INTRINSIC MOTIVATION: careers

How much of the following would the process of reaching the goal bring the client?

- ☐ feeling of making a free choice
- ☐ interest
- ☐ challenge
- ☐ enjoyment

How much would the process of reaching the goal, and the end result help meet the following needs?

- ☐ relatedness
- ☐ competence
- ☐ autonomy

EXTRINSIC MOTIVATION: careers

How much does the client agree with these statements?

- ☐ I must do it
- ☐ I should do it
- ☐ I want to do it
- ☐ It is important to me to do it

For career goals, you need to look at this both in terms of the end, and the means, for example, if a client set a goal of becoming a consultant surgeon, you would look at where the status of being such would fit, plus the roles associated with that position, and the roles that would need to be fulfiled en route (student, junior doctor etc).

GENERAL MOTIVATION: careers

How high does the client rate their own motivation?

- ☐ Globally
- ☐ Contextually
- ☐ Situationally

Give guidance by providing examples

ATTRIBUTIONS: careers

- ☐ does the client generally attribute success to internal or external factors?
- ☐ does the client generally attribute failure to internal or external factors?
- ☐ if the client has previously failed to reach this goal, do they attribute this to internal or external factors?
- ☐ are there any signs of learned helplessness, generally or specifically to this goal?

SELF-PERCEPTION: careers

- ☐ confidence - how confident is the client generally? How confident are they in the behaviours necessary to reach the goal?
- ☐ ability - do they tend towards an entity or incremental view? Do they believe they are capable of reaching the goal?
- ☐ outcome - do they believe that the planned behaviour will result in reaching the goal?
- ☐ success - do they have prior successes in similar areas they can draw from?
- ☐ imitation - there will probably be role models that they can imitate and maybe be

mentored by

- worthiness - do they feel they deserve to reach the goal?
- persuasion - is there anyone persuading them to reach the goal? If so, do they perceive this as helpful or not?
- Shavelson - chunk down the Social, Emotional and Academic domains of self-perception to find areas where the client feels particularly confident, or the opposite. This will give you the information you need to be specific in terms of encouraging their self-confidence
- Harter - look at the client's perception of competence/adequacy on the following: sociability, job competence, adequate provider, intelligence,as appropriate. This gives you more information on which to build.

ATTITUDE: careers

- beliefs - how does meeting the goal fit the client's belief system?
- emotions - what emotions are linked to both success and failure in reaching the goal?
- behaviour - how does the client's current behaviour assist or hinder the process of reaching the goal?
- others - do others have an influence on the process of reaching the goal?
- habit - work habits can be examined to ascertain if any are interfering or if any can be set to assist

PHYSIOLOGY: careers

- ☐ what physical feelings, if any, are associated with both the client's current position and the intended position on reaching the goal?

- ☐ if relevant, does the client have sufficient knowledge of the physiological processes involved?

ENVIRONMENT: careers

- ☐ in what ways may the client's physical and social environment affect the process of moving towards their goal?
- ☐ when the goal is reached, will there be any conflict with their physical or social environment?

PROs and CONs: careers

Assist the client to draw up a list of all the pros and cons of achieving the goal. For each, ascertain:

- ☐ the perceived severity (how good or bad it will be)
- ☐ the perceived probability of this happening
- ☐ how much effect the behaviour is likely to have to increase/reduce (as appropriate), the severity and/or likelihood of the outcome

Examine:

- ☐ approval and gains for the client
- ☐ approval and gains for others
- ☐ disapproval and losses for self
- ☐ disapproval and losses for others

Case example: careers

Sally is a high-flying accountant with a leading accountancy firm. She is 48 years old and is feeling unfulfilled in her work. She is divorced and her children are at University; she is tired of working all hours just to come home to an empty house. She is seeking help to find the motivation to do something about her situation. She is worried that if she carries on she could become ill or seriously depressed.

GOAL:

Sally's goal is vague. She wants to find fulfilment, but doesn't know how. This is the first of our case examples in which motivational hypnotism cannot be undertaken straight away. How can we assist Sally if she doesn't know what she wants? She says she wants to find motivation. Motivation to do what though? At the moment we need to concentrate on helping her to choose her path. She defines this as deciding whether to stay where she is and put up with it ("the money is good"), move to another firm, which may be an accountancy firm or not ("that might be like going from the frying pan into the fire"), set up on her own ("might be lonely"), or seek a different lifestyle altogether ("I've always wanted to teach tap dancing and judo to children").

Therefore, to start with we used the NLP techniques, "Keys to an Achievable Outcome" with all four scénarios, which resulted clearly in a decision not to stay where she is, but Sally felt unable to make any further decision, and was very anxious about the process. Regression was then utilised to discover the reasons for her reluctance to choose, and when this was resolved her choice became clear. She decided to go part time, start up her dance/judo school part time and aim to quit her job entirely within 18 months. However she is still fearful, and finds excuses for not taking action.

Direction: Sally's goal is both strongly towards fulfilment and contentment and away from stress and dissatisfaction

Value: Sally puts a high value on the emotions that she is directed towards.

Difficulty: she does not believe that the processes involved will be very difficult, but getting herself to do it is the hard part. She is confident in her abilities to set up the school and to market it well, and she has the financial resources required.

Identity: Sally realised when discussing this issue, how much her identity has been associated with her job throughout her adult life. It feels hard to let this go, and there is a concern as to how she will be perceived in her new role (and how she will perceive herself).

Barriers: Sally's procrastination is her primary barrier, with the fear that drives it.

Support: Sally has the support of her children in her move. Her daughter has offered to help by setting up a website, and her son has said he will decorate her premises.

The goal is specific, measurable, adjustable (in terms of logistics), realistic and time oriented.

CONTROL:

Locus of control: Sally's locus is consistently internal.

Specifically: internal. Sally is aware that she is fully in control of whether she achieves her goal or not.

INTRINSIC MOTIVATION:

There is a high degree of intrinsic motivation with this goal. Achieving it will increase Sally's feelings of making a free choice, it will be interesting, enjoyable and a challenge. It will also help her feeling of autonomy and she is looking forward to the rather different dynamics of relating to children and their parents compared to high-flying accountants and their clients.

EXTRINSIC MOTIVATION:

Sally is at the integrated regulation end of this continuum, although she also stated that all the statements were true: she feels she must do this for her health, she should do it for all sorts of reasons and she really wants to.

GENERAL MOTIVATION:

Global: recently her motivation to do anything has been very low.

Contextual: there have been no contextual areas lately where motivation has been other than low.

Situational: here her motivation is growing.

ATTRIBUTIONS:

Generally, Sally attributes both success and failure to internal factors. One exception is her recent dissatisfaction at work which she attributes to increased pressure due to restructuring at work, the increased use of technology and a bullying Chief Executive.

However, Sally attributes her failure to do anything about her situation to her own weaknesses (fear, laziness, procrastination).

SELF-PERCEPTION:

Confidence: Sally is confident when in certain roles; work, dancing or doing judo. She is only confident in social situations if they are attached to these roles. She feels that she will enjoy the social interaction that may ensue from taking more of a community role.

Ability: this is not a particular factor here. Sally already has the abilities required, just not sufficient belief and motivation to make the changes.

Outcome: Sally does believe that if she makes the changes she will find what she is looking fo:; fulfilment and contentment.

Success: she can look back at career progressions to see that she was not always an "unmotivated procrastinator". In looking at the differences, Sally realised that fear was the biggest factor. In the past she was more fearful of not striving than of going for it and failing. In this situation she had an underlying fear of losing what she had striven for even though it was no longer what she wanted.

Imitation: Sally had a colleague who gave up city life altogether to live in the country, making a living from a small herb garden. She stated "if she can do that, I can certainly do this!"

Worthiness: this question did not make much sense to Sally. She perceives it as a drop in status, so not something that there is much to be worthy of. When reframed to ask if she felt she was worthy of feeling fulfiled and content she agreed that she was.

Persuasion: no one is persuading Sally; in fact her boss is trying to dissuade, but Sally perceives this as helpful as she wants to get away from his pressure.

Shavelson:

- Social: in this domain, Sally feels particularly confident when in her work role, or dancing or doing judo. This confidence is useful for her new career as she can combine the two and in effect multiply the confidence.
- Academic: although at first glance Sally thought her academic ability was irrelevant, she realised that her confidence in her business skills would hold her in good stead for setting up her school (she had taken this for granted).
- Emotional: Sally is not too comfortable with feelings, but finds it easiest to express herself through dance. Realising this confidence increased her motivation to enable children to express their feelings in this way too.

Harter:

- Sociability: competent in the right areas
- Job competence: more than adequate
- Provider: adequate
- Intelligence: highly competent

ATTITUDE:

Beliefs: there is a clash in terms of Sally's belief in the importance of status at work. Rationally she knows that she has achieved and it is now right for her to step back, but the conflict is still there.

Emotions: there are many positive emotions linked to achieving this goal, but there remains that nagging feeling of doing something wrong by not staying in her high-powered job. The emotions connected with failing to achieve the goal are strongly negative in that Sally is concerned about her mental health if she were to remain in post.

Behaviour: Sally's current behaviours when not at work are hindering her progress, but on answering this question she realised that at work she is still able to get all that she has to do, done on time and accurately.

Others: her children will have a positive influence, as will the children who attend her school when she starts up part time.

Habit: Sally believes that she has got into a habit of being unmotivated. During her sessions so far she has realised that this is a defence mechanism that is no longer required and she is working to get over it. She is finding that taking long walks is helping to energise her as well as to give her time to think things through and plan her future.

PHYSIOLOGY:

Physical feelings: there are positive physical feelings associated with reaching the goal, namely the benefits of the dance and judo. There are also the negative effects of adrenaline associated with her current situation.

Knowledge: Sally understands the processes well.

ENVIRONMENT:

Both physical and social environments are suitable for working towards this goal, and will improve when it has been achieved.

PROS:

- Autonomy: very good and very likely
- Fulfilment: very good and very likely
- More energy: very good and very likely
- Better relationships: good and likely

CONS:

- Loss of status: somewhat bad and likely

There are many gains for Sally, and some for her children in that they are keen to see their mother more settled so that they do not have to worry about her. She realises that she will have approval from the pupils and their parents, and she suddenly realised that this would be more powerful than the supposed approval she had from being a successful accountant. The only loss to others is for her firm, but she is happy with this!

Intervention:

This information was used to create the following suggestions (please note we are not giving the specific wording so as not to unduly influence you. Each hypnotist needs to complete this process in their own style):

- Guided imagery of Sally having partially and then completely achieved her goal. Create images of her teaching, incorporating all the positive feelings (for her and the children); build in the expressiveness of dancing. Contrast with the feelings of work.

- Discuss the processes en route, how to keep focussed and to cope with setbacks.

- Use interventions to encourage her to leave the habit of procrastination behind, emphasising the positives of taking action and the good feelings associated. Particularly work with the benefits that she is experiencing from exercise. Help her to realise that procrastination is not "all or nothing", and that she can occasionally put something off for a short while when this is of benefit.

- Emphasise the intrinsic benefits (autonomy, relatedness, competence, interest, enjoyment, challenge)

- Utilise the new awareness of the status that Sally will receive via her approval from her pupils and their parents. Contrast with the status that she has now which is no longer appropriate.

- Highlight how the goal fits her value system.

- Examine Sally's identity and tie this in positively with her new role, and the emotions that she will experience.

- Continue ego-strengthening work and map past successes, and current work skills over to the new situation.

- Use future pacing to leave behind the symptoms of stress and experience the physical and emotional feelings of success. Also encourage her perception of her confidence in her new role by combining the work confidence with that of dancing and judo.

- Utilise Sally's model (colleague with the herb garden)

Personal development
Relationships

GOAL: relationships

In this section we will concentrate on relationships as in life partners, but there is no reason why this could not be used for someone who is struggling with friendships, work relationships or familial relationships.

Relationship goals are usually to get one, or to improve the one the client currently has.

- ☐ direction - movement will probably be simply towards a fulfiling relationship and away from the pain of a bad one or not having one. Variations are always possible
- ☐ value - how important is meeting the goal? Does it fit with the client's value system?
- ☐ difficulty - how hard does the client feel it will be to achieve?
- ☐ identity - is the client's identity integral to having this or another relationship, or not having one at all (eg the confirmed bachelor)?
- ☐ barriers - what obstacles are perceived by the client, and do you see any others that they have missed?
- ☐ orientation -usually not relevant
- ☐ support - support may be relevant here, perhaps a current partner wants things to be better too
- ☐ SMART - Fitting relationships to the SMART acronym can be difficult. Just bear this in mind and work with what elements you can

CONTROL: relationships

- ☐ where is the client's typical Locus of Control?
- ☐ specifically for this goal, where is their Locus of Control?
- ☐ how much control do they perceive they have over their behaviour and the outcome of that behaviour?
- ☐ how realistic do you feel their perceptions to be?

INTRINSIC MOTIVATION: relationships

How much of the following would the process of reaching the goal bring the client?

- ☐ feeling of making a free choice
- ☐ interest
- ☐ challenge
- ☐ enjoyment

How much would the process of reaching the goal, and the end result help meet the following needs?

- ☐ relatedness
- ☐ competence
- ☐ autonomy

EXTRINSIC MOTIVATION: relationships

How much does the client agree with these statements?

- ☐ I must do it
- ☐ I should do it
- ☐ I want to do it
- ☐ It is important to me to do it

In the area of relationships, there can be a strong "must" or "should" feeling. Pressure to stick with a relationship, or to have one can be immense.

However, this is a key element that can be worked on: to help the client to move towards the healthier end of the continuum, perhaps in addition to keeping hold of the "must" or "should".

GENERAL MOTIVATION: relationships

How high does the client rate their own motivation?

- ☐ Globally
- ☐ Contextually
- ☐ Situationally

Give guidance by providing examples

ATTRIBUTIONS: relationships

- ☐ does the client generally attribute success to internal or external factors?
- ☐ does the client generally attribute failure to internal or external factors?
- ☐ if the client has previously failed to reach this goal, do they attribute this to internal or external factors?
- ☐ are there any signs of learned helplessness, generally or specifically to relationships?

SELF-PERCEPTION: relationships

- ☐ confidence - how confident is the client generally? How confident are they in building relationships generally?
- ☐ ability - do they tend towards an entity or incremental view? Do they believe they are capable of making any changes necessary?
- ☐ outcome - do they believe that the planned behaviour will result in reaching the goal?
- ☐ success - do they have prior successful relationships they can draw from?
- ☐ imitation - they will know of people who have successful relationships that they can model. However it is common for people to naturally model their parents relationship, but this may not be the most appropriate model for your client
- ☐ worthiness - do they feel they deserve to have a fulfiling relationship?
- ☐ persuasion - is there anyone persuading them to reach the goal? If so, do they perceive this as helpful or not?

- Shavelson - chunk down the Social, Emotional and perhaps Physical domains of self-perception to find areas where the client feels particularly confident, or the opposite. This will give you the information you need to be specific in terms of encouraging their self-confidence
- Harter - look at the client's perception of competence or adequacy on the following: sociability, nurturance, physical appearance, adequate provider, morality, intimate relationships as appropriate. This gives you more information on which to build.

ATTITUDE: relationships

- beliefs - how does having a good relationship fit the client's belief system?
- emotions - what emotions are linked to both success and failure in reaching the goal?
- behaviour - how does the client's current behaviour assist or hinder the process of reaching the goal?
- others - consider the roles of others: not just the partner (if there is one)
- habit - habits can interfere with having a good relationship, but they would usually need to be dealt with separately

PHYSIOLOGY: relationships

- what physical feelings are associated with both the client's current position and the intended position on reaching the goal?
- does the client have sufficient knowledge of the physiological processes involved?

ENVIRONMENT: relationships

- in what ways may the client's physical and social environment affect the process of building a fulfiling relationship?
- when the goal is reached, will there be any conflict with their physical or social environment?

PROs and CONs: relationships

Assist the client to draw up a list of all the pros and cons of achieving the goal. For each, ascertain:

- the perceived severity (how good or bad it will be)
- the perceived probability of this happening
- how much effect the behaviour is likely to have to increase/reduce (as appropriate), the severity and/or likelihood of the outcome

Examine:
- approval and gains for the client
- approval and gains for others
- disapproval and losses for self
- disapproval and losses for others

Case example: relationships

Bruce has been married for thirty years and over the last two his wife, Jean, has become more and more distant. He feels that he is losing her. They do not argue, but do not communicate much in other ways either. Bruce states that he still loves Jean and wants things to improve, but spends most of his time at work or on the golf course so as to avoid the uncomfortable feelings. Jean has not worked since she was made redundant ten years ago, and both are happy with this arrangement. They have no children.

GOAL:

Bruce's goal is to regain the closeness that he once had with Jean.

Direction: the goal is towards positive feelings of love, closeness, security and contentment and away from the uncomfortable feeling of distance and inadequacy that he feels now.

Value: Bruce places a high value on his marriage ("I am not the sort to just walk away, or think the grass is greener elsewhere").

Difficulty: he believes that, while not "difficult" as such, the process will require a lot of effort and consistent hard work.

Identity: Bruce views himself very much as a "married man" and his role of husband has been "the most important role I have had".

Barriers: one potential barrier to success is Jean herself. Bruce really does not know what she wants out of the relationship, if anything.

Support: at this stage, Bruce does not know if Jean will support him in his aims to improve their marriage. There is no other support. He has lots of friends at the golf club but doesn't talk to them about this issue.

The goal is difficult to fit to the SMART acronym. Feelings are rarely specific or measurable, but discussion of these concepts helped Bruce realise that he could set goals for activities and behaviours that could assist him in reaching his overall goal, such as time spent with Jean in joint hobbies or how often he helped her with some of the household tasks that she dislikes. Bruce believes the goal to be realistic ("it must be!") and as to time, he wants to sort this sooner rather than later ("later may be too late").

CONTROL:

Locus of control: at work and on the golf course, Bruce has an internal locus of control, but at home he feels he handed all the power to Jean when she stopped work.

Specifically: in terms of the relationship he feels the control is split. He feels it was Jean's choice ("not conscious") to pull away (although he thinks it must be his fault (see attributions)), but that he hasn't done anything to influence her as yet to pull back.

INTRINSIC MOTIVATION:

The goal is inherently intrinsically orientated, but most of the measures do not apply. However, enjoyment and relatedness are very strong motivators for Bruce.

EXTRINSIC MOTIVATION:

Bruce feels that he must do this because his value system would be damaged were his marriage to fail, but he also feels that he wants to and that is important to him as a person. He feels that he will get his needs met better, that Jean will get her needs met better and they will be able to grow as a couple if he does what he is setting out to do.

GENERAL MOTIVATION:

Global: generally Bruce is reasonably motivated.

Contextual: his motivation in his home life has diminished since Jean stopped work. There is little impetus for him to do much.

Situational: he is developing more motivation to act on this situation as he realises how bad his situation may become if he does not act now.

ATTRIBUTIONS:

Generally, Bruce attributes his successes to external factors and failures to internal ones. This, he acknowledges, often leads to him being "grumpy". Specifically with regard to his marriage, he feels that it was down to Jean that they got together in the first place and that things have worked as well as they have all this time. He now blames himself for the situation.

These attributions are not particularly helpful to Bruce's situation. Finding appropriate responsibility levels and helping Bruce to reframe some other negatives could help the overall problem. For example if Bruce regularly returns from golf grumpy, this could partially explain her withdrawal.

SELF-PERCEPTION:

Confidence: Bruce is not particularly confident in any situation. He states that the place where he always felt best was at home with Jean. Now this has been replaced by work and the golf club, although he still doesn't feel very comfortable in those situations. He does not feel hugely confident in relationships generally although he says his work and family relationships, and friendships are "ok".

Ability: Bruce believes that he has all the abilities required to make this change and that it is simply a question of making a choice and then applying himself to it fully and consistently and avoiding the temptation of hiding away in future.

Outcome: he is hopeful that the planned behaviours will produce the desired outcome but Bruce is not certain.

Success: Bruce can draw on the earlier success of his marriage.

Imitation: he does not want to look at other successful relationships as he feels that they are bound to be different to his, and he wants to be true to himself. The possible benefits were not laboured as he was adamant.

Worthiness: Bruce feels that he, and "more importantly" Jean , deserve this outcome.

Persuasion: no one is influencing Bruce in his endeavour.

Shavelson:

- Social: Bruce feels at his most confident currently when tending to his roses (first mention of this hobby!). He says that this is something that he knows he can do, and that he gets approval for (from Jean and others). He is at his least confident when playing golf against a visiting club when their players have a much lower handicap, or at the office when his work is being inspected.
- Emotional: Bruce does not generally express emotions. He finds it easiest to express resentment and frustration ("not anger itself, or anything soppy"). It is much easier to shut off.
- Physical: when asking this question, Bruce mentioned his sex life for the first time, stating that it was not particularly important but it would be nice to get things going again on that front. He said that "that was for later, now I just want to get on".

Harter:

- Sociability: close to adequate
- Nurturance: used to be adequate, but no longer
- Physical appearance: adequate
- Provider: competent
- Morality: competent
- Intimate relationships: used to be adequate, but no longer

ATTITUDE:

Beliefs: marriage is central to Bruce's belief system.

Emotions: Bruce feels that if he succeeds in his goal he will feel happier, more settled and secure, more content and less guilty. If he does not succeed in reaching his goal, he says that he will feel sad, ashamed and lonely.

Behaviour: his current behaviour of avoidance will hinder any progress, but he has decided that it is this behaviour that needs to change.

Others: Jean's role is critical, but Bruce does not feel that anyone else has a role to play.

Habit: on raising this issue, Bruce revealed that he drinks what Jean believes to be too much. Bruce believes it to be a reasonable amount and states that he never gets drunk, and that this is a cause of dissension between them. He is unwilling to address this issue at present, saying that if things get better perhaps Jean will be more tolerant.

ENVIRONMENT:

Bruce's physical and social environments will be supportive of his moves towards the goal. They have a nice home where they have always been comfortable together, and have access to attractive places to visit, which they used to enjoy doing together. Socially they do little and have tended to rely on each other, which Bruce believes can only be beneficial in the circumstances.

PROS:

- Positive emotions: very good and very likely
- Moving away from negatives: very good and very likely

CONS:

There are no cons.

Bruce perceives these gains to be for both himself and Jean, and that there are no losses.

Intervention:

This information was used to create the following suggestions (please note we are not giving the specific wording so as not to unduly influence you. Each hypnotist needs to complete this process in their own style):

- Guided imagery to assist Bruce to see things as they could be, incorporating positive emotions. Also, use of time line to look back, and forwards comparing the good times with the not so good, and a positive future.

- Encourage the behaviours decided upon, strengthening the positives, and building belief and commitment.

- Highlight the ways the goal, and the process fit his value system.

- Utilise ego-strengthening to aid with problem areas, and map the confidence associated with his roses to other areas as highlighted by Shavelson.

- Boost his feeling of control, and work with the unhelpful attributions, helping him to take appropriate responsibility.

Overcoming anxiety

GOAL: anxiety

In this section we include generalised anxiety, phobias, nervous conditions and panic disorder. It may seem strange to some readers that clients would not be motivated to conquer anxieties, but this an area where secondary gain is particularly common.

Goal-setting for anxiety issues is not always easy: often the client will just say they want to feel better. Do what you can to help define exactly what they want and don't want.

- ☐ direction - is movement required towards something or away from something?
- ☐ value - how important is meeting the goal? Does it fit with the client's value system?
- ☐ difficulty - how hard does the client feel it will be to achieve?
- ☐ identity - is the client's identity integral to behaviour as is, or as will be? Look for secondary gain
- ☐ barriers - what obstacles are perceived by the client, and do you see any others that they have missed?
- ☐ orientation -usually not relevant
- ☐ support - does the client have support in making this change?
- ☐ SMART - is the goal
  Specific ?
  Measurable ?
  Adjustable?
  Realistic?
  Time-based?
  Note that the goal may not be to remove all anxiety, but to cope better and reduce it. We will use the term "deal with their anxiety" to cover these possibilities

CONTROL: anxiety

- ☐ where is the client's typical Locus of Control?
- ☐ specifically for this goal, where is their Locus of Control?
- ☐ how much control do they perceive they have over their attempt to deal with their anxiety?
- ☐ how realistic do you feel their perceptions to be?

INTRINSIC MOTIVATION: anxiety

How much of the following would the process of dealing with their anxiety bring the client?

- ☐ feeling of making a free choice
- ☐ interest
- ☐ challenge
- ☐ enjoyment

(the latter three are unlikely)

How much would the process of reaching the goal, and the end result help meet the following needs?

- ☐ relatedness
- ☐ competence
- ☐ autonomy

EXTRINSIC MOTIVATION: anxiety

How much does the client agree with these statements?

- ☐ I must do it
- ☐ I should do it
- ☐ I want to do it
- ☐ It is important to me to do it

GENERAL MOTIVATION: anxiety

How high does the client rate their own motivation?

- ☐ Globally
- ☐ Contextually
- ☐ Situationally

Give guidance by providing examples

ATTRIBUTIONS: anxiety

- ☐ does the client generally attribute success to internal or external factors?
- ☐ does the client generally attribute failure to internal or external factors?
- ☐ if the client has previously failed to deal with their anxiety, do they attribute this to internal or external factors?
- ☐ are there any signs of learned helplessness, generally or specifically to do with their anxiety?

SELF-PERCEPTION: anxiety

- ☐ confidence - how confident is the client generally? Where exactly do they lack confidence?
- ☐ ability - do they tend towards an entity or incremental view? Do they believe they are capable of dealing with their anxiety?
- ☐ outcome - do they believe that their plans will result in reaching the goal?
- ☐ success - do they have prior successes in similar areas they can draw from?
- ☐ imitation - do they know of anyone who has dealt with their sort of anxiety? If not you can use surface structure metaphor to assist
- ☐ worthiness - do they feel they deserve to overcome their anxiety?
- ☐ persuasion - is there anyone persuading them to act? If so, do they perceive this as helpful or not?
- ☐ Shavelson - chunk down the domains of self-perception that are relevant to their particular anxiety to find areas where the client feels particularly confident, or the opposite. This will give you the information you need to be specific in terms of encouraging their self-confidence
- ☐ Harter - look at the client's perception of competence or adequacy on whichever domains are appropriate.

ATTITUDE: anxiety

- ☐ beliefs - how does dealing with their anxiety fit the client's belief system?
- ☐ emotions - what emotions are linked to both success and failure in dealing with their anxiety?
- ☐ behaviour - how does the client's current behaviour assist or hinder the process of reaching the goal?
- ☐ others - do others have an influence on the process of reaching the goal?
- ☐ habit - if a habit is to be broken, how strong does the client perceive it to be? Do they have a tendency towards being habitual?

PHYSIOLOGY: anxiety

- ☐ what physical feelings are associated with both the client's current position and the intended position on reaching the goal?
- ☐ does the client have sufficient knowledge of the physiological processes involved?

ENVIRONMENT: anxiety

- ☐ in what ways may the client's physical and social environment affect the process of moving towards their goal?
- ☐ when the goal is reached, will there be any conflict with their physical or social environment?

PROs and CONs: anxiety

Assist the client to draw up a list of all the pros and cons of achieving the goal. For each, ascertain:

- ☐ the perceived severity (how good or bad it will be)
- ☐ the perceived probability of this happening
- ☐ how much effect the behaviour is likely to have to increase/reduce (as appropriate), the severity and/or likelihood of the outcome

Examine:

- ☐ approval and gains for the client
- ☐ approval and gains for others
- ☐ disapproval and losses for self
- ☐ disapproval and losses for others

Case example: anxiety

Jenny is a 19 year old administrative assistant who seeks help with anxiety and blushing. She struggles at work as she spends most of her time worrying that someone will talk to her, and she avoids any social situation outside the home (she lives with her parents). She has two good friends and she can go shopping with them, but nothing else.

GOAL:

Jenny has not thought in terms of setting goals: she just wants to "feel better", not to blush and to be able to live her life. Using subjective units of distress she rated her anxiety at 9 out of 10 at work, and 3 out of 10 at home, and 4 out of 10 when shopping. She says that to go out socially with her friends would be like a rating of 20.

From this point she was able to set the following goals for the next month:
Work: 5
Home: 1
Shopping: 1
Going out: to begin to believe it may be possible

Direction: this is more of an away from goal than we have seen in previous cases. Jenny wants to get away from the anxiety and stress that she feels, but of course she also wants to move towards "life". Jenny finds it difficult to identify what it will be like as she is so wrapped up in the negatives, and like most people who suffer from anxiety, the fear of the anxiety.

Value: Jenny sees resolution of her problems as "worth more than the world". In fact it has such a high value that this adds to her doubts as to possibility.

Difficulty: she sees this as very difficult to achieve: "I have done everything I can". She believes that hypnosis can help, but before therapy she was feeling that this was because the therapist would be changing her. Part of what was required was to help her realise that this is a "do with" process, not a "do to" process, and that this makes it more powerful, not less.

Identity: Jenny has an identity of "shy", and the blushing also seems to be a part of her identity too in that she relates it to be common for people to say she is blushing before she does. At first glance secondary gain is not obvious although as sessions progress this may emerge.

Barriers: the key obstacle is Jenny's lack of belief in herself and her ability to change. This question prompted Jenny to say "I am useless". She does not like herself and feels that others therefore shouldn't like her either.

Support: Jenny has good support in making this change. Her parents are encouraging as is her boss who has told Jenny that she has great potential in the company if she would "open up". Her boss is happy with Jenny's work despite the fact that she herself feels so distracted.

The goal is has been made as specific and measurable as seems reasonable at this time. It is adjustable, realistic and time oriented. Jenny may build in other goals as she goes along, such as to go to certain places or talk to certain people.

CONTROL:

Locus of control: Jenny has a generally external locus of control. She states that she has felt controlled all her life and that she has never had a chance to make her own decisions. However, the thought of being in control is frightening.

Specifically: at work, Jenny rarely takes the initiative, nor does she control much about her environment at home. When shopping with friends she says "I go where they want".

INTRINSIC MOTIVATION:

Jenny feels that by consulting a hypnotist she is making a free choice, which in itself is a step towards control. She said that she is motivated to find interest, challenge and enjoyment and that they will be more likely if the anxiety is reduced, so they are aims to reach for. Reaching the goal will help her to be more related and autonomous.

EXTRINSIC MOTIVATION:

Jenny is at the Identified Regulation point of extrinsic motivation. She really wants to sort herself out, but the doubt and conflict with current sense of self is preventing her from seeing it as Integrated.

GENERAL MOTIVATION:

Global: low

Contextual: medium; Jenny said that she would be more motivated to do things if she did not fear them so much.

Situational: she is quite highly motivated to deal with the issue

ATTRIBUTIONS:

Generally, Jenny attributes success and failure externally. This goes along with the control aspects of her situation. She takes little responsibility for anything in her life, but does recognise that if she were to feel better she could make a difference to herself. There are signs of generalised learned helplessness. It seems to be a "choice" to view herself as hopeless, pathetic and unlikeable.

SELF-PERCEPTION:

Confidence: her confidence is generally low; she couldn't find an area of life where she felt confident. At home, she feels "ok".

Ability: Jenny tends towards an entity view. This contributes to her lack of confidence at work. She does fine there, but Jenny cannot take any credit for this. She doubts her ability to deal with her anxiety.

Outcome: Jenny is hopeful that the hypnotic interventions will help her to achieve her goal, but she is sceptical.

Success: she claims not to have prior successes. When questioned about successes at school, she reported good exam results and some success in swimming, but she discounted these experiences.

Imitation: Jenny says that no one she knows experiences anxiety like she does.

Worthiness: she does not feel worthy of success or happiness, but wants to!

Persuasion: no one is specifically persuading her to take action, but her parents, boss and friends are supportive. Jenny perceives this as helpful, but not terribly relevant. "What good can they do?"

Shavelson: we did not look at the domains as I had already got the picture that Jenny was not willing to find areas of confidence at this time.

Harter: unusually here, I left out what might be considered more relevant domains (such as sociability), so as not to go over negative ground again, and specifically asked for the perception of others in most cases.

- Job competence: J's view: adequate, boss would say competent
- Nurturance: J's view: adequate (in caring for little sister), parents would say competent
- Athletic abilities: J's view: adequate (swimming), coach would say competent
- Physical appearance: J's view: adequate, friends would say more than adequate
- Morality: competent
- Intelligence: J's view: adequate, teachers would say competent
- Sense of humour: better than adequate

ATTITUDE:

Beliefs: Jenny couldn't see any connection between her beliefs and this issue

Emotions: if she is able to leave these problems behind, Jenny says she will be able to find happiness and fulfilment. For the first time, she expressed a slight excitement at the possibility! She said that if she gets nowhere, she will just feel the same as she does now which is "awful but at least it's familiar".

Behaviour: Jenny's current behaviour is not helping her in that she has a tendency to hide and remain in the shadows whenever possible. However, she does go shopping with her friends, and she does go to work consistently (even if she "hides" when she is there), so there are things to work on.

Others: apart from the support mentioned previously, there was just one area where Jenny perceived an influence: those who tease her for blushing.

Habit: Jenny thinks that perhaps her tendency to withdraw is habitual, and not always necessary or appropriate.

PHYSIOLOGY:

Physical feelings: the physical feelings involved arise from the adrenaline reaction

Knowledge: Jenny's knowledge of the fight or flight response is limited and she had not realised that this is what was happening

ENVIRONMENT:

Jenny's physical environment has little relevance, except that her open-plan office will assist her in her moves to avoid hiding. Her social environment, while very limited is supportive, and her friends are happy for her to go out with them to pubs etc as well as shopping so safe possibilities exist for exploration.

She does not expect any conflicts if the goal is reached.

PROS:

- Opportunity for success at work: good and likely
- Possibility of getting a boyfriend: very good and very likely
- Happiness: very good and possible

CONS:

- "huge risks" to take: very bad and very likely

If Jenny is to overcome her anxiety it will result in considerable gains for herself, and potentially for others in that she will not need so much support and Jenny feels she will "be able to give more". She will also potentially gain some approval, but she cannot perceive of any losses or disapproval for herself or others.

Intervention:

This information was used to create the following suggestions (please note we are not giving the specific wording so as not to unduly influence you. Each hypnotist needs to complete this process in their own style):

- Guided imageryto assist Jenny to see herself as a confident, outgoing person, who feels comfortable in any situation (be careful not to make this TOO strong). Incorporate visualisations of all the situations discussed, such as work, home, shopping and begin to add in a little of the idea of socialising with friends.

- Work on building an awareness of possibility, and on the idea of incremental views for the relevant behaviours and abilities.

- Help Jenny to choose appropriate behaviours to adopt in place of the previous tendency to hide.

- Strengthen her belief in herself, her right to find fulfilment, and her abilities as already demonstrated at work, in swimming, and the good perceptions of the others around her.

- ☐ Work with the perception of risk if she is to "put herself out there", and how to deal with anyone who teases her.

- ☐ Enhance both towards, and away from aspects.

- ☐ Tie Jenny's identity in with the new way of being and disconnect from old ways.

- ☐ Utilise ego-strengthening techniques.

- ☐ Boost feelings of control: look at areas where she does have control (simple things such as the fact that she decides what to wear each day), and extend.

- ☐ Encourage Jenny to attribute any successes, however small, internally, and look at past successes too in this way.

- ☐ Educate her about the fight/flight response so that she understands what is happening to her body.

- ☐ Assist Jenny to be aware that set-backs will occur and give her tools and self-belief to deal with them

Medical issues
Serious illness

GOAL: serious illness

The process of defining the goal can be a complex and difficult process for clients with serious illness, but this alone can be beneficial.

A hypnotist can work with a client with serious illness in terms of survival and/or quality of life. It must be recognised that for some serious illness sufferers will not survive whatever interventions occur.

- direction - a client is likely to be moving away from death and suffering, and/or towards life, acceptance, receptiveness to treatment etc. Both can be maximised
- value - how important is it for the client to survive the disease or at least assist in their treatment and improve their quality of life? In what ways does it fit, or not, their lifestyle? How can you use this in your intervention?
- difficulty - how hard does the client feel it will be to survive the disease or assist in its treatment?
- identity - is the client's identity integral to being survivor, or perhaps to being ill? How can you help them see themselves positively?
- barriers - what obstacles are perceived by the client, and do you see any others that they have missed?
- support - does the client have support in their struggle?
- SMART - the goal is specific, measurable, realistic (for some this will not be the case as far as survival, but can be with regards to improving quality of life), and time-based (this can be determined by external factors of the disease)

CONTROL: serious illness

- ☐ where is the client's typical Locus of Control? Does the client feel that they have a level of control over their life?
- ☐ specifically for this goal, where is their Locus of Control? Does the client feel that they have a level of control over the disease?
- ☐ how much control do they perceive they have over their treatment?
- ☐ how much do they feel that their serious illness means an inevitable death?
- ☐ how realistic do you feel their perceptions to be? Do you need to work with these?

NB: it is not your role to determine true levels of control or predict outcomes. You and your client need to work with conventional medicine, and to acknowledge expertise.

INTRINSIC MOTIVATION: serious illness

By becoming a survivor of serious illness, or working to improve their quality of life, the client is likely to:

- ☐ get a feeling control
- ☐ perceive it as a challenge
- ☐ not expect the process to be enjoyable (so emphasise the enjoyable elements of being a survivor and the treatment)

Becoming a survivor can help the client

- ☐ feel empowered: they are achieving something vital
- ☐ gain autonomy: disease no longer controls them

EXTRINSIC MOTIVATION: serious illness

How much does the client agree with these statements?

- ☐ I must do it
- ☐ I should do it
- ☐ I want to do it
- ☐ It is important to me to do it

GENERAL MOTIVATION: serious illness

How high does the client rate their own motivation?

- ☐ Globally
- ☐ Contextually
- ☐ Situationally

Give guidance by providing examples

ATTRIBUTIONS: serious illness

- ☐ does the client generally attribute success to internal or external factors?
- ☐ does the client generally attribute failure to internal or external factors?
- ☐ if the client has previously had family or friend survive serious illness, do they attribute this to internal or external factors?
- ☐ are there any signs of learned helplessness, generally or specifically to serious illness treatment?

SELF-PERCEPTION: serious illness

- ☐ confidence - how confident is the client generally?
- ☐ ability - do they tend towards an entity or incremental view? Do they believe they are capable of becoming a serious illness survivor or if that is not possible of improving their quality of life?
- ☐ outcome - using the reasons they have stated for wanting to meet their goal, how strongly do they believe that they will meet it and how much do they perceive that their participation in the treatment will produce the desired result?
- ☐ success - do they have prior successes in similar areas they can draw from? Maybe overcoming other illnesses or injury?
- ☐ imitation - do they know of anyone who has achieved the goal? You can use surface structure metaphor here.
- ☐ worthiness - do they feel they deserve the outcome they are looking for?
- ☐ persuasion - is there anyone persuading them to reach the goal? If so, do they perceive this as helpful or not?
- ☐ Shavelson - chunk down the Social domain of self-perception to find areas where the client feels particularly confident, or the opposite. Do the same with the Emotional domain. This will give you the information you need to be specific in terms of encouraging their self-confidence
- ☐ Harter - look at the client's perception of competence or adequacy on the following: Sociability, Nurturance, Appearance, Provider, Intimate Relationships. More information on which to build

ATTITUDE: serious illness

- ☐ beliefs - how does meeting this goal fit the client's belief system?
- ☐ emotions - what emotions are linked to both success and failure in meeting this goal? Obviously in this instance you need to be prepared for strong emotions
- ☐ behaviour - how do other behaviours assist or hinder the process, eg diet, smoking, exercise? (NB Only give advice that you are qualified to give)
- ☐ others - do others have an influence on the process? Eg doctors or family

PHYSIOLOGY:serious illness

- ☐ what physical feelings are associated with both the client's situation and how they intend to be? This may include the physical effects of medical interventions
- ☐ does the client have sufficient knowledge of the physiological processes involved?

ENVIRONMENT: serious illness

- ☐ in what ways may the client's physical and social environment affect the process?

PROs and CONs: serious illness

Assist the client to draw up a list of all the pros and cons of achieving the goal. For each, ascertain:

- the perceived severity (how good or bad it will be)
- the perceived probability of this happening
- how much effect the behaviour is likely to have to increase/reduce (as appropriate), the severity and/or likelihood of the outcome

Examine:

- approval and gains for the client
- approval and gains for others
- disapproval and losses for self
- disapproval and losses for others

Case example: serious illness

Leonard was a 65 year old gentleman who presented for assistance with cancer. The treatment was an adjunct to his conventional cancer treatment. The information gathering process elicited the following significant points:

GOAL:

Direction: Leonard was keen to move towards better health so that he could see his sons get married, and away from the death and the fear of the unknown leading from that.

Value: he did feel that surviving the cancer was very important, but also thought that the treatment he was receiving had very little value as it was causing him great pain and inconvenience for what seemed little benefit.

Difficulty: he had no doubts that the road ahead would be difficult

Identity: Leonard was diagnosed with cancer at 64, so his identity had changed from a virile man to now being a "sick old man".

Barriers: Leonard felt that the biggest hurdle was the fact that several members of his family did not survive cancer, so the barrier was psychological.

Support: he had solid support from all his family

CONTROL:

Locus of control: Leonard had spent 40 years working as a driver then a supervisor for an international delivery company and had responsibilities for others for 20 of those years, first as a shop steward then as a supervisor. He was a man of action and was used to giving instructions. His family life was run according to his instructions, his wife Mary died 20 years previously and was responsible for both bread-winning and acting as mother and father to two of his sons. Leonard seemed to have control over most aspects of his life.

Specifically: Leonard believed that the only person who could get him through this was him.

He did not believe that death was the inevitable result of his disease, but he admitted to the fact that this was the first time since the death of his wife he felt that things were out of his control.

I opted to use several metaphorical examples of how much control he actually has.

INTRINSIC MOTIVATION:

Leonard perceived that to become a survivor would be a challenge. He did not expect the process to be enjoyable but he thought that the end result of being a survivor would be.

EXTRINSIC MOTIVATION:

Leonard chose the third option, the Identified level.

GENERAL MOTIVATION:

Global: high

Contextual: high for his children, as well as high for his retirement, which he worked very hard to achieve at the age of 63.

Situational: medium

ATTRIBUTIONS:

He recited several things that he had succeeded at in his life and attributed these to a mixture of internal and external factors. Most of it was work related, but he felt that before his wife had died, that he was not the best of fathers, he believed that he learned to be a good parent although it had not always been easy.

SELF-PERCEPTION:

Confidence: High

Ability: An able man, but concerned that his personal family history may work against him

Outcome: Leonard strongly believed that surviving cancer would give him the outcomes he sought.

Success: Leonard felt that he was in part to blame for his condition and was prepared to take responsibility for that. He took great pride in being able to get out of "fixes" in the past and was hopeful that he could get out of this "cancer fix"

Imitation: his father and three brothers died of cancer, he certainly was not intending to meet their fate. He did not have anyone to model for survival

Worthiness: he felt completely worthy of his intended outcomes

Persuasion: No external persuasion

Shavelson: Leonard feels particularly confident with his colleagues from his old depot and his family. Emotionally, Leonard was ok with most emotions and at several times in the session expressed the range of emotions one would expect to have when diagnosed with cancer. He said he did not like to cry, but found himself doing quite a bit of that of late.

Harter:

- Sociability: better than adequate
- Nurturance: competent
- Appearance: Very important to him, still exercised 3 times a week and never leaves the house without a tie.
- Provider: adequate
- Intimate relationships: very close with his children

ATTITUDE:

Beliefs: being a cancer survivor fitted well into his belief system of needing to be in control of his destiny. He values his family highly.

Emotions: Leonard had very little difficulty in expressing his emotions and though at first apprehensive he was able to touch the deep fears he has towards the failure of his treatment.

Behaviour: other behaviours seemed to be in alignment with his survival, although he is finding the change in diet to be of a particular challenge.

PHYSIOLOGY:

Physical feelings: Leonard experienced great pain and discomfort on days he was receiving chemotherapy, also he had felt physically weaker since the treatment commenced.

Knowledge: Leonard knew a great deal about the physical processes of the orthodox treatment of cancer he had been receiving.

ENVIRONMENT:

Home seemed as though it would be supportive and enabling with no conflicts to mention

PROS:

- Survival: very good and likely
- Seeing children and grandchildren: very good and likely
- Enjoy the rest of his retirement: very good and likely

CONS:

- Pain and discomfort: very bad and likely
- Lethargy and listlessness: bad and likely
- Irritability: bad and likely

The approval for himself would come from himself and his family. The gains for himself would be survival and retirement enjoyment. For others the gains would be to have him around and losses are none. For himself, losses are temporary, and only relevant during the treatment.

Intervention:

This information was used to create the following suggestions (please note we are not giving the specific wording so as not to unduly influence you. Each hypnotist needs to complete this process in their own style):

- Guided imagery of Leonard feeling happy and proud as he sees his children get married and eventually the birth of grandchildren. Also include physical feelings with comments on speed of the cancer being destroyed and that his cells rejuvenate and his body becomes stronger.

- Use phrase "it is important to you" to move him from identified to integrated extrinsic motivation level.

- Discuss relatedness that will be gained, feelings of achievement, challenge (but do-able, liken to his previous career progression), feeling empowered and strong

- Build on intrinsic motivation: health, love of family, retirement enjoyment. Stress ability to achieve goals, that he has no other bad habits.

- Discuss family values and his role as provider and nurturer.

- Use future pacing to see himself getting over the obstacle of his treatment and how strong and healthy he was now that the cancer had been dealt with. Reinforce happiness and pride at being in control of his body

- Stress all pros and minimise cons (explain pain and discomfort as well as lethargy can be assisted with use of hypnosis)

- Everything about becoming a survivor is positive and will feel good.

- Reinforce idea that he can have the identity of being the member of his family to beat cancer

- Raise awareness of how lifestyle changes to diet etc can assist in this process.

- Using the Shavelson info, discuss areas where he is confident and how those where he isn't are not necessarily down to his abilities. Map positive to the negative and future pace

- Stress positives from Harter: sociability, children, nurturing and providing

Medical issues:
Surgery/injury

GOAL: surgery/injury

The goal is to improve recovery times and decrease discomfort. The process will involve continuing practice of self-hypnosis

- ☐ direction - movement is towards health and comfort and away from pain, illness and discomfort
- ☐ value - health is often a significant part of a person's value system, either in a positive or potentially negative way
- ☐ difficulty - how hard does the client feel it will be to achieve?
- ☐ identity - is the client's identity connected to the health issue concerned? For example, a young woman having a hysterectomy may struggle with then being unable to have children
- ☐ barriers - what obstacles are perceived by the client, and do you see any others that they have missed?
- ☐ support - does the client have support in this?
- ☐ SMART - this goal may well be difficult to be fit the acronym, but SUDS may help

CONTROL: surgery/injury

- ☐ where is the client's typical Locus of Control?
- ☐ specifically for recovery, where is their Locus of Control?
- ☐ how much control do they perceive they have over their situation and the outcome of the processes involved?
- ☐ how realistic do you feel their perceptions to be?

INTRINSIC MOTIVATION: surgery/injury

It is unlikely that a recovery process is going to involve very much intrinsic motivation. However there could be aspects of a challenge, and possibly autonomy

EXTRINSIC MOTIVATION: surgery/injury

Extrinsic motivation needs to be considered somewhat differently to the usual way for this situation.

GENERAL MOTIVATION: surgery/injury

How high does the client rate their own motivation?

- ☐ Globally
- ☐ Contextually
- ☐ Situationally

Give guidance by providing examples

ATTRIBUTIONS: surgery/injury

- ☐ does the client generally attribute success to internal or external factors?
- ☐ does the client generally attribute failure to internal or external factors?
- ☐ if the client has previously experienced similar situations, did they attribute their recovery experience to internal or external factors?
- ☐ are there any signs of learned helplessness, generally or specifically recovery?

SELF-PERCEPTION: surgery/injury

- ☐ confidence - how confident is the client generally? How confident are they in any behaviours and processes necessary to reach the goal?
- ☐ ability - do they tend towards an entity or incremental view? Are there behaviours they do not feel able to do which would help?
- ☐ outcome - do they believe that their plans will result in reaching the goal?
- ☐ success - do they have prior successes in similar areas they can draw from?
- ☐ imitation - do they know of anyone who has received the benefits they are striving for? Do you?
- ☐ worthiness - do they feel they deserve to recover quickly and with less discomfort?
- ☐ persuasion - is there anyone persuading them to work on this? If so, do they perceive this as helpful or not?
- ☐ Shavelson - chunk down the Emotional domain of self-perception to find areas where the client feels particularly confident, or the opposite. This will give you the information you need to be specific in terms of encouraging their self-confidence
- ☐ Harter - look at the client's perception of competence or adequacy on the applicable domains. More information on which to build

ATTITUDE: surgery/injury

- ☐ beliefs - how does making a good recovery fit the client's belief system?
- ☐ emotions - what emotions are linked to both success and failure in making a good recovery?
- ☐ behaviour - how does the client's current behaviour assist or hinder the process?
- ☐ others - do others have an influence on the process?
- ☐ habit - if a habit is to be broken, how strong does the client perceive it to be? Do they have a tendency towards being habitual?

PHYSIOLOGY: surgery/injury

- ☐ what physical feelings are associated with both the client's current position and the intended position on reaching the goal?
- ☐ does the client have sufficient knowledge of the physiological processes involved?

ENVIRONMENT: surgery/injury

- ☐ in what ways may the client's physical and social environment affect the process of making a good recovery?
- ☐ when they have recovered, will there be any conflict with their physical or social environment?

PROs and CONs: surgery/injury

Assist the client to draw up a list of all the pros and cons of achieving the goal. For each, ascertain:

- the perceived severity (how good or bad it will be)
- the perceived probability of this happening
- how much effect the behaviour is likely to have to increase/reduce (as appropriate), the severity and/or likelihood of the outcome

Examine:

- approval and gains for the client
- approval and gains for others
- disapproval and losses for self
- disapproval and losses for others

Case example: surgery/injury

Peter has been involved in a car accident in which his left femur was badly broken necessitating surgery to pin the bone. There was also considerable soft tissue damage in addition to that caused by the surgery itself. He is a "reasonably healthy and fit" man of 37. His surgeon has said that he will be in plaster for at least six weeks and that full mobility is unlikely to return within a year, "if at all". Peter is feeling very low and is in a lot of pain. He is the owner/manager of a garden centre and as he cannot go to work he is worried about how the business will survive without him.

GOAL:

Peter's goal is to speed up his recovery, to reduce his pain and to "enjoy" his convalescence.

Direction: the goal is towards health and comfort and away from pain, discomfort and the worries and depression he is currently feeling.

Value: Peter values his health very highly. Although he describes himself as "reasonably healthy and fit", it is clear that he has high standards. He is used to running three times a week and going to the gym twice a week. He reports a very healthy diet and states that he is a non-smoker who's only vice is "the odd glass of wine".

Difficulty: the next few months are hanging over Peter's head and the thought of getting through it seems very difficult.

Identity: Peter's identity is highly related to his health and lifestyle, including his job.

Barriers: Peter does not perceive any extra barriers to his progress other than the injuries themselves.

Support: Peter has the support of his wife and young children who he says have been doing a great job trying to keep his spirits up. He says it is helping his relationship with his 9 year old twins as he has begun reading the Harry Potter books to them. He is already on the second and expects to get all the way through by the time he is ready to return to work!

The goal has been made as specific and measurable as is possible, using SUDS. It is adjustable, realistic and time oriented. Peter has also set specific goals for other activities, such as the amount of reading (his own interests as well as Harry Potter), studying (he is taking the opportunity to learn Spanish) and physiotherapy exercises.

CONTROL:

Locus of control: Peter has an internal locus of control in most situations. In discussion he recognised that this was a problem in terms of being able to hand over responsibility for this business, even though he trusts his employees.

Specifically: in terms of his recovery, Peter feels more of an external locus. He feels that he has been "prodded and poked" and that "his body is no longer his own".

INTRINSIC MOTIVATION:

He sees his recovery as a challenge and this is why he is seeking help. He recognises that he can maximise the time and find ways to help himself if he can leave the negative feelings behind.

EXTRINSIC MOTIVATION:

Peter is motivated by the thought of getting better and recovering his life as he knows it. There are extrinsic aspects, and it is a highly integrated goal.

GENERAL MOTIVATION:

Global: high

Contextual: for health, high

Situational: high, although brought down at times by the negative emotions.

ATTRIBUTIONS:

Generally, Peter attributes both success and failure internally. He is finding it difficult to reconcile the external locus of control with regard to his injury with this way of being as they seem to conflict. He feels that he needs to take control, and thus to be able to attribute the results internally. He is clear that the accident itself was attributable to external sources: he was hit by a car that had experienced acute brake failure. However, he harbours no animosity to the driver of the other car who he says "did all he could to control the car".

SELF-PERCEPTION:

Confidence: generally Peter is a confident person, but he is aware that he restricts himself to environments where he feels ok to avoid any feelings of doubt.

Ability: this did not seem relevant to Peter.

Outcome: he firmly believes that if he applies himself he can achieve his aim

Success: he claims not to have had any prior successes in this area. He has always been fit and well and has never had surgery or a serious injury before. That, he says, is why this has "knocked him for six".

Imitation: Peter has, of course, seen people overcoming injuries, but the case that sticks in his mind is of his mother's problems following a riding accident when a dislocated shoulder did not heal properly. His fear is that he will experience the same thing.

Worthiness: I did not ask this question as it was clear that Peter was very clear on his right to get better and back to work quickly.

Persuasion: he describes those around him as supportive rather than pushy, and feels grateful for their support. He says that his wife, in particular is being very patient with him.

Shavelson: Peter's confidence is good in most areas of the emotional domain. He says that he is happy to express feelings, and has done so a lot in the current situation. He does not block how he is feeling, and lets it show, "perhaps a little too much". The one area of doubt was of how it is to be "incapable". He finds the idea of depending on people problematic, and feels this is a contributory factor to his current mood.

Harter: in this case, we looked at domains which were affected by the issue:

- Sociability: at the moment Peter is unable to do much in the way of socialising and is missing this in his life
- Job competence: he is having to run his business from a distance, which is causing some problems
- Nurturance: he is getting more of an opportunity to nurture his family which is definitely good for him
- Athletic abilities: he is concerned as to how much these will be affected long term

- Physical appearance: Peter does not like the fact that he will be scarred quite severely, and permanently
- Adequate provider: he worries as to his potential in business long term, "should things go wrong"

ATTITUDE:

Beliefs: Peter has a strong belief in the importance of a healthy lifestyle, so his aims fit well.

Emotions: these are clearly delineated. If he recovers well there are many strong positives, and if not there are many strong negatives. The latter also applies to the current situation, and the projections of the surgeon.

Behaviour: Peter's previous healthy lifestyle choices will undoubtedly help his recovery. He feels fine about incorporating physiotherapy into his daily routine, and is used to scheduling his time.

Others: he knows he can rely on those around him to help him with practicalities.

Habit: Peter says that his activity habits have been habitual, as have his working practices. He says he just needs to "jig them around a bit".

PHYSIOLOGY:

Physical feelings: there are many physical feelings that Peter is not used to; the pain, of course, from the leg, but also knock on effects of being immobilised and the effects of medication. He stated that if he had thought of this scenario before it happened he would not have realised that he would feel so "ill".

Knowledge: Peter says that he knows "enough" about the physiology involved. He asks a lot of questions of his doctors and reads up on any medication he is given.

ENVIRONMENT:

His environment is helpful in that he feels comfortable at home. It will be a while before he will be mobile at all, and then the stairs will present "a challenge, not a problem". His family provides a stable social environment.

PROS:

- Good health: very good and very likely
- Increased feelings of autonomy: good and likely

CONS: none

The gains for himself and others are self-evident. The quicker he can recover the better for all concerned. Peter feels he will get approval from those around him if he does well, but cannot see any negatives at all.

Intervention:

This information was used to create the following suggestions (please note we are not giving the specific wording so as not to unduly influence you. Each hypnotist needs to complete this process in their own style):

- Guided imagery to allow Peter to experience comfort and ease as he recovers, including imagery of the emotions he wants to find, and the activities he intends to involve himself in. Encourage him to see himself speaking Spanish, reading to his children, benefiting from his physiotherapy, and enjoying the processes.

- Work on acceptance of how things are, and will be, but also build in expectation of progress.

- Encourage intrinsic motivation for the chosen behaviours, moving him towards an Integrated regulation for each activity.

- Following discussion look at a reward programme, if that is what Peter feels would be right.

- Strengthen his beliefs in the process of recovery, utilising surface and deep structure metaphors.

- Highlight how health and fitness are integral to Peter's beliefs and values system and reframe the current situation emphasising the learning that can take place and the strength that Peter can develop from the experience.

- Help Peter to recognise that his situation is different from his mother's and that he has more control over his recovery than he or the doctors are currently giving him credit for.

- Encourage regular use of self-hypnosis, building belief and understanding of the benefits.

- Work with the pluses in the environment to build feelings of comfort, safety and well-being, and use ego-strengthening too to help Peter leave behind the feelings of depression and start to view the outlook positively.

- Address the issues raised by examining the Harter domains.

- Work with possible set backs and future pace to successful recovery.

- Utilise pain control techniques, only with full support and permission of Peter's doctors.

Special considerations

Children

All the techniques and ideas described in this book can be utilised with children, but only if you are qualified to work with them! Most hypnotism qualifications in the UK and US are designed to enable you to work with adults, not children, so we recommend that if this is an area that interests you, that you take a specialist certification in this area.

If you do use Motivational Hypnotism with children, it is crucial that you find a balance between sounding too technical, and sounding patronising; this is not always an easy balance to find. Many of the concepts that we use in this model would be difficult for a child to grasp. For example if you attempted to explain the difference between intrinsic and extrinsic motivation to a 10 year old, it may (or may not!) prove difficult. Of course some of these ideas may be a stretch for some adult clients too.

The crucial thing is to think through your questioning strategies and develop your method of using this with whichever client group you are working with. It does not matter if a client does not understand the term "attribution", for example: they will know what you mean if you ask them "who was responsible for that?" or "why did that happen?".

Psychiatric conditions and pain

Most professional hypnotists are not qualified to work with psychiatric conditions or to diagnose. If in doubt, always ask for a written medical referral and if you get one and are still in doubt, refer the client to someone who is qualified to treat.

If a client presents with any symptoms of pain, a medical referral must be received before it is safe to work with this.

Ethical practice

At the time of writing there is no regulation for the practice of hypnotism in the UK, and regulation varies from state to state in the USA. It may be lawful for you, where you live to set up in practice without a proper qualification, but this, we believe is unethical and will not serve you well long term.

If you are not already qualified, we recommend that you take a course that meets one or both of the following criteria:

- leads to the award of the Hypnotherapy Practitioner Diploma in the UK. This diploma is awarded by various schools through the National Council for Hypnotherapy and NCFE. For more information visit www.hypnotherapists.org.uk
- leads to membership of the National Guild of Hypnotists in the USA. For a list of the NGH's Certified Instructors, visit www.ngh.net

Professional practice does not just rely on qualification, but adherence to a suitable Code of Ethics provided by such organisations such as the National Council for Hypnotherapy (UK) and the National Guild of Hypnotists (US). Two particular areas to note are the need for regular Continuing Professional Development and for professional support, such as supervision.

Marketing

Now that you are beginning to understand the model of Motivational Hypnotism, we expect that you will be able to see that this opens up a new angle in terms of your potential market. Who wouldn't benefit from your help?!

For any service to be effective, there need to be the following elements:

- A provider
- A service
- A customer

This may seem obvious (and indeed it is), but all these factors are crucial in creating success. You need to work to make yourself the best provider you can possibly be and work to make your service the best it can be. Not only must these two elements be the best, they must also be what the customer wants, and the customer must know they want the benefits you offer.

This is good news! There are lots of areas to work on, and if you do so, you will succeed. However, there are many therapists who dislike that word "work". If you are one of them, here is a suggestion for you: how about using Motivational Hypnotism on yourself?

We can break the elements down further to:

- Being the best therapist you can be
- Providing the best service you can
- Letting your clients know you are there
- Letting your clients know they need you

When beginning to think about setting up your Motivational Hypnotism practice, while all are important, the latter is the particular challenge, as potential clients are unlikely to think of hypnotism as a source of assistance.

Income Formula

Let us introduce you to the first of our formulae. This was created by the authors to illustrate the elements that seem to contribute to the amount of income that is received by anyone undertaking any role.

There may well be exceptions to this rule but we have not, as yet, found any.

Income	=	value	x
		difficulty	x
		rarity	x
		image	x
		number of users	

The "number of users" element of the formula needs an explanation immediately as this may not be obvious. By this we mean someone who benefits from what the provider does. This may be direct or indirect. For example a best selling novelist will have millions of users who benefit from their work, while a surgeon will have few users as it is normal to operate on only one person at a time.

To illustrate this formula let's look at some examples:

H=High, M=Medium, L=Low

	Value	Difficulty	Rarity	Image	N Users	Income
David Beckham*	H	H	H	H	H	H++++
Plumber	H	M	M	M	L	M
Nurse	M	M	M	L	L	L
Cleaner	L	L	L	L	L	L

To explain, the perceived value of what Beckham does for his "users" is high, as is that of the plumber (you really need that washing machine!). Beckham might not find what he does difficult but most would, and few are so good at it. There are things which are rare but not difficult (eg being a sagger maker's bottom knocker), or difficult but not rare (eg counselling).

*David Beckham is captain of the English soccer team and a style icon.

Image comes into the equation too. There are other footballers with the same level of skill etc. as Beckham, but without the glamour. They might come in at M or L on image and the resulting income would be that much lower.

The image of the role itself is also a factor. For example, it could be argued that the actual work done by an air steward is very similar to that of a waitress, but one has a much higher image than the other. Finally the number of users impacts greatly on income. Take the example of the nurse. A nurse can only look after so many people at one time, and this limits the income dramatically, whereas David Beckham's skills are enjoyed by millions.

So, how does this affect you in your role as a Motivational Hypnotist? Simply that you have the opportunity to work to maximise each element of the formula.

Maximising the "N users" element might be possible for those who choose to do group work. However, you may prefer to work one to one and not too many hours, and so concentrate your efforts on the other elements. The image of hypnotism varies from country to country, but there is always the opportunity to work on this through the way you behave and market yourself.

And remember, most of these elements are perceptions, and it is the perceptions of your "users" that need to be maximised. It can be very useful to ask friends and colleagues about their perceptions of all these factors, and of you too, if you dare!

The Success Formula

One more formula: this is designed (again by the authors) to show the elements required in a process to have a successful outcome:

Success	=	goal	+
		movement	+
		resources	-
		obstacles	

If we use a soccer analogy, success (scoring), requires a goal (literally), movement of the player, resources (ie a ball) and an absence of obstacles (ie players of the other team) OR getting round the obstacles.

In terms of your Motivational Hypnotism practice, let's look at each of these elements:

Goal: if you don't know where you are going, you probably won't get there. Therefore you need to set targets. What does success mean to you in the short and long term?

Movement: that means you doing things, taking action and not just sitting, waiting for clients to drop metaphorically into your lap.

Resources: things such as books, the Internet, journals, colleagues, and professional societies, all of which can assist you in achieving success

Obstacles: these can be internal or external. For example, fear of success and lack of knowledge are internal obstacles, and lots of competition and inappropriate premises are external obstacles.

For further information on marketing, see

"Building a Successful and Ethical Therapy Practice"

***by Shaun Brookhouse and Fiona Biddle,* ISBN 0-9544604-0-5**

Future Developments

The concept of Motivational Hypnotism as described in this book is a new one, although based on tried and trusted theories. We are intending to develop the ideas further, and would be interested in any feedback of how you find working with the concepts. Also if you have any suggestions for areas of development we would be happy to hear from you.

To contact us, please email info@ukacademy.org

Looking forward to hearing from you!

Further Reading

Ajzen, I. & Fishbein, M. (1980) Understanding attitudes and predicting social behaviour. Englewood Cliffs, NJ: Prentice Hall

Ajzen, I. (1988) Attitudes, personality and behaviour. Milton Keynes: Open University Press

Bandura, A. (1977) Self-efficacy: toward a unifying theory of behavioral change.. Pychological Review, 84: 191-215

Bandura, A. (1986) Social foundations of thought and action: A social cognitive theroy. Englewood Cliffs, NJ: Prentice Hall

Brookhouse, S. & Biddle, F. (2002) Building a Successful and Ethical Therapy Practice. Loughborough: UK Academy of Therapeutic Arts and Sciences Ltd.

Deci, E. & Ryan, R. (1985) Intrinsic motivation and self-determination in human behavior. New York: Plenum Press

Dweck, C. (1992) The study of goals in psychology. Psychological Science, 3: 165-7

Godin, G. (1994) Social-cognitive models. In R. Dishman (Ed), Advances in exercise adherence (pp. 113-36). Champaign, Ill.: Human Kinetics

Harter, S. (1978) Effectance motivation reconsidered: Toward a developmental model. Human development, 21: 34-64

Harter, S. & Connell, J. (1984) A model of children's achievement and related self perceptions of competence, control and motivational orientations. In J. Nicholls (Ed) Advances in motivation and achievement. III. The development of achievement motivation (pp. 219-50). Greenwich, Conn.: JAI Press

Heap, M. & Aravind, K. (2002) Hartland's medical and dental hypnosis, fourth edition. Edinburgh: Churchill Livingstone

Hovland, C. & Rosenberg, M. (Eds) (1960) Attitudes, organisation and change: An analysis of consistency among attitude components. New Haven, Conn: Yale University Press

Janz, N. & Becker, NM. (1984) The Health Belief Model: A decade later. Health Education Quarterly, 11: 1-47

Lewis, F. & Daltroy, L. (1990) How causal explanations inflence behavior: Attribution theory. In K. Glanz et al (Eds), Health behavior and health education (pp. 92-114) San Francisco, Calif: Jossey-Bass

Maehr, M. & Braskamp, L. (1986) The motivation factor: A theory of personal investment. Lexington, Mass.: Lexington Books

Maehr, M. & Nicholls, J. (1980) Culture and achievement motivation: A second look. In N. Warren (Ed) Studies in cross-cultural psychology (vol II pp 221-67). New York: Academic Press

Maddux, J. (1993) Social cognitive models of health and exercise behaviour: An introduction and review of conceptual lissues. Journal of Applied Sport Psychology, 5: 99-115

Prochaska, J. & DiClemente, C. (1983) Stages and processes of self-change in smoking. Towards an integraive model of change. Journal of Consulting and Clinical Psychology, 51: 390-95

Rogers, R. (1983) Cognitive and physiological processes in fear appeals and attitude change: A revised theory of protection motivation. In K. Cacioppo & R. Petty (Eds), Social psychology: A sourcebook (pp 152-76). New York: Guildford Press

Rosenstock, I. (1990) The Health Belief Model: Explaining health behavior through expectancies. In K. Glanz et al (Eds), Health behavior and health education (pp. 92-114) San Francisco, Calif: Jossey-Bass

Rotter, J. (1966) Generalised expectancies for internal versus external control of reinforcement. Psychological Monographs, 80 1-28

Shavelson, R. et al. (1976) Self-concept: Calidation of construct interpretations. Review of Educational Research, 46: 407-41

Skinner, E. (1995) Percieved control, motivation and coping. Thousand Oaks, Calif: Sage

Triandis, H. (1977) Interpersonal behaviour. Monterey, Calif: Brooks/Cole

Vallerand, R. (1977) Toward a hierarchical model of intrinsic and extrinsic motivation. In M. Zanna (Ed), Advances in experimental social psychology (vol 29, pp 271-360). New York: Academic Press

Weiner, B. (1979) A theory of motivation for some classroom experiences. Journal of Educational Psychology, 71: 3-25

Index

The UK Academy offers:

- Continuing Professional Development courses for hypnotists and others
- Training in Hypnotherapy (through our sister school, WSCAH (see www.hypno-nlp.org)
- An ezine, Inspirations. Just email us via info@ukacademy.org and ask for this, and it will arrive in your inbox every 10 days

To download a prospectus and for further information, visit

www.ukacademy.org

Printed in the United Kingdom
by Lightning Source UK Ltd.
116908UKS00001B/337